SURPRISING HISTORY STORIES TO TICKLE YOUR BRAIN

E. D. Garner

CONTENTS

SURPRISING HISTORY STORIES TO TICKLE YOUR BRAIN

By E.D. Garner

AN APPLE A DAY? TRY KETCHUP INSTEAD!

Early European colonists in America believed that tomatoes were poisonous when they were first introduced to the red-hued fruit. This misconception came from a few different beliefs. They thought tomatoes were tainted because they looked like other poisonous plants, like deadly nightshade. Also, there were rumors about people getting sick or even dying after eating tomatoes, which added to the fear.

Moreover, because tomatoes are acidic, they could react with lead, often found in pewter dishes and utensils in Europe and early America. This added to the idea that tomatoes were terrible for you.

Although it's hard to say precisely where the idea that tomatoes were "red with the blood of the poor souls who ate them" came from, it was probably an exaggeration based on fears about eating tomatoes during the period. Of course, these beliefs didn't last forever. Over time, as tomatoes became a common ingredient in many recipes, people realized they weren't poisonous, and the myth faded away.

During the 1830s, tomato ketchup, consisting of tomatoes, vinegar, and assorted spices, was thought to possess medicinal benefits. It was advertised as a universal remedy for various health problems, such as digestive troubles, rheumatism, and diarrhea.

In 1834, an Ohio physician named John C. Bennett began marketing tomato ketchup as a remedy, asserting its ability to alleviate conditions such as rheumatism and diarrhea. Collaborating with pill manufacturer Archibald Miles, Bennett produced pill forms of his tomato ketchup, dubbed "Extract of Tomato." This pseudo-medicine gained widespread popularity, with newspapers reporting anecdotes of ketchup users experiencing relief from various ailments.

Early ketchup recipes varied greatly, with some not even including tomatoes. Some ketchup versions use ingredients like mushrooms, walnuts, and fish. Despite variations in ingredients, ketchup was promoted as a health remedy and stocked in pharmacies alongside other medicinal items. As competition grew, some ketchup vendors made even bolder claims than Bennett, asserting that their tomato pills could heal broken bones and more. However, studies conducted by independent researchers found no evidence to support these assertions. Consequently, after 15 years without tangible results, public interest in medical ketchup waned—nevertheless, the popularity of ketchup as a condiment persisted.

In 1876, Heinz entered the market with ketchup, which quickly gained traction as a popular condiment made from tomatoes, distinct from its previous medicinal use. Initially, the company focused on producing and selling horseradish, vinegar, and pickles. A pivotal factor in the success of Heinz ketchup was Henry J. Heinz's innovative packaging approach. That same year, Heinz unveiled the iconic clear glass bottle with a narrow neck, enabling customers to see the product's quality. This transparent packaging became synonymous with Heinz ketchup and set it apart from competitors.

In 1904, the company introduced its iconic slogan, "57 Varieties," despite offering over 60 products. This clever marketing tactic highlighted Heinz's dedication to quality and variety.

Ketchup holds the title of the most beloved condiment in the United States. It has been a fundamental part of American culinary culture for years, serving as a go-to topping or dipping sauce for various dishes, from hamburgers and hot dogs to fries and sandwiches. Americans collectively consume billions of pounds of ketchup annually, solidifying its reign as the reigning champion of condiments in the country. While other condiments like mustard, mayonnaise, barbecue sauce, and hot sauce also enjoy popularity, ketchup consistently holds the top spot in terms of both consumption and preference among Americans.

THE SHORTEST WAR IN HISTORY LASTED ONLY 38 MINUTES!

T he Anglo-Zanzibar War is renowned as one of history's briefest armed conflicts, spanning just 38 minutes on August 27, 1896. Although short-lived, this confrontation between the British Empire and the Sultanate of Zanzibar carries considerable historical weight, offering insights into colonial power dynamics, imperial aspirations, and the quest for autonomy in East Africa during the late 19th century.

Zanzibar, situated in the Indian Ocean off the coast of East Africa, comprises multiple islands, including the primary ones of Unguja, often called Zanzibar Island, and Pemba Island. It is integrated into the United Republic of Tanzania and lies approximately 25-50 kilometers (16-31 miles) from mainland Tanzania. Renowned for its strategic positioning, Zanzibar has historically served as a vital hub for trade, notably in spices, ivory, and enslaved people. British dominion was established over

Zanzibar during the late 19th and early 20th centuries. This status as a British protectorate was formalized in 1890 following the Heligoland-Zanzibar Treaty, which delineated spheres of influence in East Africa, with Zanzibar falling under British jurisdiction while Germany acquired territories on the mainland, such as Tanganyika, now part of Tanzania.

Fundamentally, the Anglo-Zanzibar War emerged due to mounting tensions arising from Britain's growing colonial pursuits in Africa and the Sultanate's struggle to maintain autonomy in the face of increasing European influence. The conflict was sparked by a succession crisis triggered by the unexpected demise of Sultan Hamad bin Thuwaini. Upon assuming the role of Sultan of Zanzibar on July 25, 1896, Sultan Khalid bin Barghash staunchly resisted British authority and rebuffed their demands for submission to their imperial dictates.

Sultan Khalid's rule, although brief, was marked by turmoil and upheaval. On August 25, 1896, he asserted his claim to the Sultanate in defiance of the British administration's selection of Sultan Hamoud bin Mohammed as his successor. The tension escalated dramatically when Sultan Khalid's troops, positioned at the Beit al-Hukm (the Sultan's palace), initiated an attack on the British consulate, prompting a rapid and resolute retaliation from the British forces.

Under Rear Admiral Harry Rawson's leadership, the British Royal Navy unleashed a barrage of firepower upon the palace, swiftly overpowering the Sultan's defenses and compelling an immediate surrender. This pivotal event triggered the Anglo-Zanzibar War, which was famously one of the shortest conflicts on record, lasting 38 minutes. After the war, Sultan Khalid sought sanctuary in the German consulate but ultimately yielded to British authorities. Consequently, he faced exile from Zanzibar, residing in enforced seclusion until his demise in 1927.

The aftermath of the Anglo-Zanzibar War carried significant implications, marking the erosion of its self-governance and shift towards British oversight as a protectorate. The treaty ratified following the conflict installed a sultan favorable to British interests and extended their authority over Zanzibar's governance and economy, firmly establishing British hegemony in the region.

Moreover, the Anglo-Zanzibar War starkly illustrates the unequal power dynamics inherent in colonial interactions. It underscores the extent to which imperial powers would go to protect their interests and assert dominance over native lands.

Although brief, the Anglo-Zanzibar War left a lasting impact, providing valuable insights into the complexities of colonialism, sovereignty, and African resistance. Zanzibar achieved independence from British rule on December 10, 1963. However, this independence was short-lived as Zanzibar merged with Tanganyika on April 26, 1964, forming the United Republic of Tanzania. This union resulted from the Zanzibar Revolution, which toppled the Sultanate of Zanzibar and established a revolutionary government. Tanganyika had already gained independence from British rule in 1961, under the leadership of Julius Nyerere, who became the first President of Tanzania following the union.

GEORGE WASHINGTON LED FEDERAL TROOPS AGAINST WHISKEY DISTILLERS AND THEN...OPENED HIS OWN DISTILLERY.

During the early years of America, alcohol was integral to everyday life, social norms, and economic pursuits. It was widely enjoyed and firmly established in colonial society, with people of all ages and social statuses regularly partaking in various alcoholic beverages.

In early America, cider emerged as a prevalent alcoholic beverage, especially in regions abundant with apples, like New England. Often crafted at home through fermenting apple juice, cider became a staple drink enjoyed by both adults and children. Additionally, beer gained popularity and was brewed locally by households, taverns, and small breweries. It wasn't just sought after for its intoxicating properties but also for its safety, as water was frequently contaminated. Moreover, rum, derived from molasses imported from the Caribbean, found widespread consumption in early America, notably in the Caribbean colonies and along the Atlantic coast. Used in various cocktails and as a form of currency in trade with Indigenous American tribes and enslaved Africans, rum held a significant place in colonial society.

Alcohol served more than just recreational needs; it also held significance in social and religious ceremonies. Taverns had a vital role as communal spaces where individuals gathered to imbibe, socialize, and engage in business dealings.

Throughout the 1700s, alcohol remained significant in the daily lives of many individuals. It was commonly consumed during social gatherings and served various purposes, including medicinal use and as a trading commodity. George Washington held progressive views regarding alcohol consumption, adopting an enlightened approach. He savored a diverse array of beverages, with a preference for sweet, fortified wines such as Madeira and Port. Additionally, he indulged in rum punch, porter, and whiskey. While Washington acknowledged the risks associated with excessive alcohol intake, he advocated for moderation as a guiding principle.

Rye whiskey became popular because of the plentiful supply of rye grain in the northeastern United States, especially in states such as Pennsylvania and Maryland. The climate and soil conditions in this region were ideal for growing rye, making it easily accessible and cost-effective for making whiskey.

The Whiskey Rebellion, also referred to as the Whiskey Insurrection, erupted as a violent protest against taxes in the United States from 1791 to 1794 during George Washington's presidency. This uprising stemmed from the implementation of the "whiskey tax," marking the first levy imposed on a domestic product by the newly established federal government.

The transportation challenges and perishable nature of beer made rum and whiskey more favorable choices. While rum distillation in the U.S. had been disrupted during the Revolutionary War, whiskey production and consumption surged afterward, although rum still held a production edge over whiskey by 1791.

Enacted in 1791 to alleviate Revolutionary War debt, the tax was applied to all distilled spirits, but due to the growing popularity of American whiskey, it became widely known as the "whiskey tax." Frontier farmers, accustomed to distilling surplus grains into whiskey, fiercely resisted this tax, considering whiskey a vital means of trade in their communities.

Many of these farmers, veterans of the Revolutionary War, viewed the tax as a violation of the principles they had fought for, particularly the concept of taxation without local representation. Conversely, the federal government argued that the taxes were a lawful exercise of Congressional taxation authority.

In the counties of Western Pennsylvania, protestors resorted to violence and intimidation to obstruct federal officials from enforcing the tax. Tensions escalated in July 1794 when a

U.S. marshal ventured into Western Pennsylvania to serve writs on distillers who had not paid the excise. The situation reached a critical point when over 500 armed individuals launched an assault on the fortified residence of tax inspector John Neville. In response, President Washington dispatched peace envoys to negotiate with the insurgents in Western Pennsylvania while simultaneously urging governors to deploy militia forces to enforce the tax. Also, Washington led an army to quell the rebellion, accompanied by 13,000 militiamen supplied by the governors of Virginia, Maryland, New Jersey, and Pennsylvania.

Before the army's arrival, the rebels dispersed and returned home, avoiding any direct conflict. Approximately 20 individuals were apprehended, but all were either acquitted or granted pardons. Meanwhile, attempts to tax distillers in neighboring Kentucky proved exceedingly challenging, with more than 175 distillers convicted of defying the tax law in the following six years. Court records and newspaper articles document numerous instances of resistance to taxation.

The Whiskey Rebellion showcased the determination and capability of the fledgling national government to quell violent opposition to its laws, even though enforcing the whiskey tax proved challenging. These events played a role in the emergence of political parties in the United States, a trend that was already in motion. The whiskey tax was eventually repealed in the early 1800s during Thomas Jefferson's presidency. Historians contend that in the grand scheme of things, this incident bolstered American nationalism as it demonstrated the populace's admiration for Washington's adept handling of the rebels without resorting to authoritarian measures.

Following his presidency, George Washington ventured into whiskey distillation. During this phase of his life, Washington aimed to streamline his farming endeavors and downsize his extensive land holdings. Ever the entrepreneur, Washington was attracted to the profit prospects offered by a distillery. His decision to establish a substantial distilling operation reflects his commitment to adopting the most advanced and inventive farming techniques of the time. Despite lacking prior distillation experience, Washington swiftly familiarized himself with the process.

In 1797, George Washington embarked on commercial distillation, prompted by his Scottish farm manager, James Anderson, who possessed expertise in grain distillation from his experience in Scotland and Virginia. With its expansive merchant gristmill and plentiful water resources, Anderson successfully persuaded Washington that Mount Vernon's agricultural produce offered a lucrative opportunity for a distillery venture. Construction of a sizable stone still house, capable of accommodating five stills, commenced in October 1797. The foundation comprised large river rocks sourced from the Falls of the Potomac, while the distillery walls were constructed from sandstone quarried from Mount Vernon.

Washington's distillery maintained a continuous operation with five copper pot stills throughout the year, a departure from the norm where the typical distillery employed one or two stills and operated for just one month annually. In 1799, Washington's Distillery achieved an impressive production of nearly 11,000 gallons of whiskey, valued at $7,500 (equivalent to approximately

$120,000 today). By contrast, the average Virginia distillery of that era yielded around 650 gallons of whiskey annually, valued at roughly $460.

Distilleries remained prevalent in early America, as evidenced by the 1810 census, which recorded over 3,600 distilleries operating solely in Virginia. However, the widespread use of alcohol also raised concerns regarding its adverse societal impacts, including public intoxication, violence, and family breakdowns. Consequently, various temperance movements emerged in the 19th century, advocating for moderation or complete prohibition of alcohol consumption. These movements reached a climax with the enactment of prohibition laws in the early 20th century, temporarily prohibiting the sale and consumption of alcoholic beverages across the United States.

The authentic taste of George Washington's original rye whiskey recipe can be experienced today. Distilled at George Washington's meticulously reconstructed distillery in Mount Vernon, Virginia, this whiskey is crafted from a recipe uncovered by scholars poring over the distillery ledgers dated 1798 and 1799. Staying true to Washington's original mash bill and employing 18th-century techniques, the grain is processed using Washington's water-powered gristmill, then fermented in traditional wooden mash tubs before distilling in copper pot stills heated by wood fires. While whiskey during Washington's era was typically not aged, this revived recipe calls for double distillation, primarily for enhanced flavor and safety. Produced in limited quantities, this whiskey is exclusively available for in-person purchase, allowing enthusiasts to savor a piece of American history firsthand.

NONE OF THE 2,000 PEOPLE ACCUSED DURING THE SALEM WITCH TRIALS WERE BURNED AT THE STAKE

T he Salem witch trials that occurred in 1692 stand out as a grim chapter in American history, marked by fear, suspicion, and heartbreaking deaths. These trials took place in the Massachusetts Bay Colony in the modest town of Salem, Massachusetts, and its nearby regions, leaving a lasting impact on the nation's memory.

Various factors, including strong religious beliefs, social tensions, and economic uncertainty, caused the Salem witch trials. Puritanism, the dominant religious ideology at the time, significantly impacted these events. Puritanism originated as a movement within the Church of England during the 16th and 17th centuries to reform the church by eliminating what they saw as remnants of Roman Catholic practices. The Puritans stressed strict adherence to the Bible and emphasized the concept of predestination, which held that God had already determined the fate of each person, whether they would be saved or damned. This strict interpretation of religious doctrine helped to create a deeply ingrained belief in the supernatural and the existence of evil forces in the world.

The Puritans were known for upholding a lifestyle of moral rectitude and self-discipline. They followed strict guidelines and refrained from worldly indulgences. The Bible was considered the ultimate guide for matters of faith, and the Puritans aimed to construct a society rooted in biblical principles. In Puritan communities, education and literacy were highly valued, leading to establishing schools and colleges to ensure that individuals could read and interpret the Bible independently. According to Puritan beliefs, salvation was achieved through faith in God and adherence to moral principles rather than through actions alone. The Puritans emphasized the significance of personal devotion and religious commitment, striving to align their lives with God's teachings in every aspect.

Puritanism profoundly impacted the social, political, and cultural evolution of England and its colonies in North America. The Puritans played a crucial role in the colonization of the New World, establishing settlements such as Plymouth and Massachusetts Bay to create societies that adhered to their religious beliefs. These colonies became known for their strict moral codes, lack of tolerance for other religions, and emphasis on hard work and self-discipline.

Puritanism was a significant movement that had a

considerable impact on society. However, it faced opposition and criticism from various groups, including other religious denominations and secular authorities. Although its influence declined in England over time, Puritanism's legacy continued and left a lasting impression on American society, particularly in New England. Puritan values and customs significantly influenced the region's culture and institutions.

The Massachusetts Bay Colony had a strict social hierarchy, which created suspicion and unease among its community members. In January 1692, a group of young girls, including Betty Parris and Abigail Williams, began to display strange symptoms such as seizures, spasms, and visions. With no logical explanation available, the villagers turned to superstition and accused witchcraft of being the cause behind the girls' unusual behaviors, which eventually led to the Salem witch hysteria.

The town of Salem and its surrounding areas were gripped by panic, fueled by rumors, gossip, and accusations. Those accused were frequently individuals who were already marginalized in society, such as widows, social outcasts, and women who were deemed to be of questionable moral character. The populace was consumed by anxiety and distrust as claims of witchcraft spread, leading to the arrest and imprisonment of numerous innocent individuals.

The Salem witch trials were characterized by a flawed legal process that denied the accused fundamental rights and protections. To find guilty convictions, courts often relied on spectral evidence—accounts based on dreams and apparitions—while ignoring basic ideas of impartiality and equality. Witchcraft suspects faced harsh interrogations, torture, and public humiliation, which heightened the climate of mistrust and terror.

In the summer of 1692, the frenzy's zenith was reached when 20 individuals perished—19 by hanging and one by being crushed under large stones. Men, women, and even two dogs, allegedly the witches' companions, were among the victims. These deaths sent a chilling message about the consequences of unchecked frenzy and injustice throughout the colony.

Instances of burning witches at the stake were not as common in England or North America as they were in continental Europe. When such executions did occur, they were usually seen as punishment for practicing witchcraft. During the early modern era, particularly in the 16th and 17th centuries, witchcraft was viewed as a serious offense and a threat to Christian beliefs and societal order. Witches were believed to have made a pact with the Devil and used supernatural powers to harm others or communicate with evil spirits.

In some instances, particularly in continental Europe, the witchcraft trials were supervised by nonreligious authorities who utilized torture to force confessions from the accused. If a confession was obtained, the punishment for witchcraft might include hanging, drowning, or burning at the stake.

The burning of women accused of being witches at the stake served various purposes. It was thought to cleanse the soul of the accused and discourage others from engaging in witchcraft. Additionally, it functioned as a public display meant to inspire fear and maintain societal structure. Nonetheless, it's crucial to acknowledge that not all accused witches met this fate. Numerous individuals were executed through alternative methods like hanging or drowning, depending on prevailing laws and traditions. Furthermore, the witch hunts were marred by rampant injustice, with countless innocent individuals facing accusations and executions based on weak evidence or mere suspicion.

The aftermath of the Salem witch trials was characterized by regret, repentance, and efforts at making amends. In 1693, the Massachusetts Bay Colony officially recognized the mistakes and unfairness of the trials, providing compensation to the families of those affected. Nevertheless, the wounds inflicted by the trials lingered for years, serving as a warning about the perils of collective hysteria and the significance of honoring principles of fair treatment and human dignity.

THE OLYMPICS,
IN THE NUDE!

T he ancient Olympics were held in Olympia, Greece and were a significant part of ancient Greek culture. These games represented both religious reverence and athletic competition, dating back to antiquity. They were a testament to the Greeks' strong beliefs in the significance of physical fitness, the celebration of the human body, and the worship of their pantheon of gods.

Participation in the Olympics was seen as a means of seeking divine approval and blessing. The athletes, known as Olympians, trained extensively for years to prepare for the games, striving to achieve victory and glory in the name of their city-states and gods. The events encompassed various athletic disciplines, including running, wrestling, boxing, chariot racing, and the pentathlon, which combined running, jumping, discus throwing, javelin throwing, and wrestling.

During ancient Greece, participating in sports in the nude had both practical and symbolic importance, deeply ingrained in the culture and principles of the era. In the physically demanding field of ancient Greek sports, which relied heavily on agility, strength, and endurance, competing without clothing h relied heavily on agility, strength, and endurance, competing without clothing eliminated potential obstacles caused by garments. This allowed wrestlers to move more fluidly and engage with their adversaries without encumbrance. Additionally, this practice prevented opponents from using clothing as leverage during matches, promoting fair and impartial competition. It's worth noting that the term "gymnastics" originates from the Ancient Greek words "gumnasía," meaning "athletic training or exercise," and "gumnós," signifying "naked."

The Olympics were not just about competition, but also about building camaraderie and unity among the Greek city-states, which were often involved in political rivalries and conflicts. To ensure that the sanctity of the games remained untarnished by warfare, the Olympic truce allowed for a period of ceasefire that extended from one month before the games to one month after. This allowed athletes and spectators to travel to Olympia safely.

In ancient times, winning an event at the Olympics was the ultimate achievement for an athlete. Upon their return to their hometowns, victors were celebrated as heroes. They were awarded olive wreaths, which symbolized the sacred olive trees of Olympia, as a mark of their accomplishment. Poems and songs were also composed in their honor, praising their virtues.

The ancient Olympics were not free from controversies and scandals. Instances of bribery, cheating, and political manipulation were not uncommon, which reflected the intense competition and the high stakes involved in the games. However, despite these issues, the spirit of the Olympics remained intact and transcended the petty rivalries of mortal men. It affirmed the enduring legacy of the ancient Greeks' reverence for physical excellence and Bribery, cheating, and political manipulation were not uncommon, reflecting divine favor.

The ancient Olympics were a symbol of the Greeks' deep respect for the human body, the significance of athletic competition, and the value of religious devotion. These sporting events were held in honor of Zeus and other gods and were considered a sacred ritual. They were a tribute to strength, skill, and the unwavering spirit of competition. Although these games are now a part of history, the legacy of the ancient Olympics continues to inspire athletes and spectators to strive for excellence and to pay homage to the gods with every display of strength and skill.

OH THOSE KOOKY VICTORIANS

I n the Victorian era, it was common practice to take photographs of deceased loved ones. The family members would dress up their dead relatives in their finest clothes and pose them in a lifelike manner before capturing the images. The purpose of this ritual was to preserve a final memory of the deceased loved one. Photography has been used to capture memories, both joyful and sorrowful, since the 19th century.

There are several reasons why people take postmortem photos, and we will discuss some of them here. One of the main reasons, which we will focus on today, is because it is a natural human instinct to want to possess something that belonged to a loved one who has passed away. In a way, taking a photo can help mitigate the feeling of loss. While some people may find it strange to take pictures of deceased individuals in modern times, it was a common practice in the past.

During the Victorian era, postmortem photographs were not displayed openly. Instead, they were kept as personal keepsakes and stored in a locket along with a lock of the person's hair. In some cases, they were framed but kept in private places like a bedroom or a family room. They could also be small enough to fit in one's pocket.

During the Victorian era, it was a common practice to take postmortem photographs of loved ones. These photographs were also known as "memento mori," which is a Latin phrase that translates to "remember that you have to die." This phrase was used to reflect on one's mortality and was often depicted in various forms of art and literature throughout history. In the 19th century, this sentiment took on a form of sentimentality, where people would commission trinkets made from the hair of their deceased loved ones or carry a locket with a photo of them.

During the time when photography was gaining popularity and becoming more affordable, postmortem photography became a trend. This involved taking photographs of people who had passed away and was offered as a service by professional portrait photographers. Initially, this was done mostly using the daguerreotype process, which was the dominant photographic technique at the time.

The daguerreotype was a highly detailed image on polished silver that was initially a luxury item affordable only to the wealthy. However, as the number of photographers increased and production costs decreased throughout the 1840s, it became more accessible. In the 1850s, cheaper modes of photography were introduced, including the ambrotype on glass and the tintype on thin, inexpensive metal. Additionally, photographs were being printed on paper during this time. By the 1860s, portrait photography was affordable for most people.

During the Victorian era, there were high rates of mortality, specifically among infants and children, due to diseases like tuberculosis, cholera, and influenza. Consequently, postmortem photography became increasingly common among families who lost a young child. These photographs were a way to remember and pay tribute to the brief lives of those who passed away too soon.

During the Victorian era, postmortem photography was a way to cherish the memory of a deceased loved one. These photographs typically depict the person as if they were sleeping or resting peacefully. Children were often photographed in small coffins and surrounded by flowers. These pictures were taken shortly after death, sometimes even before the funeral. Although some may find these photographs eerie, they are a display of love and sentimental sadness. For families, photography provided a physical and visual means of confronting and processing their grief.

THE FIRST AMERICAN MEDAL OF HONOR WAS BESTOWED DURING THE CIVIL WAR

T he first American Medal of Honor was granted on March 25, 1863, amidst the American Civil War. Private Jacob Parrott from the 33rd Ohio Infantry was the recipient, honored for his bravery during the Andrews Raid, commonly called the Great Locomotive Chase, which unfolded on April 12, 1862.

A team of Union soldiers, under the guidance of civilian scout James J. Andrews, penetrated Confederate territory to sabotage the crucial Western & Atlantic Railroad, a vital supply route for the Confederate forces. Andrews and his comrades, posing as civilians, boarded a northbound train in Marietta, Georgia. Their objective was to hijack the locomotive, named the General, and disrupt Confederate communication and supply channels by destroying tracks, bridges, and telegraph lines as they journeyed northward toward Chattanooga, Tennessee.

The raid began as intended, with the Union soldiers managing to seize the General and assume train command. Nonetheless, they encountered numerous obstacles, such as delays provoked by Confederate pursuit and the need to dismantle railroad tracks. As Confederate forces became aware of the situation, they initiated a pursuit, requisitioning additional locomotives to track down the stolen train.

The pursuit spanned around 87 miles (140 km) and endured for several hours, during which the crew of the General, under the guidance of engineer William Allen Fuller, executed audacious tactics to impede and outmaneuver the pursuing Confederates. However, the Union raiders faced insurmountable challenges that thwarted their mission, including fuel depletion and the abandonment of the General after it became immobile due to steam exhaustion.

Confederate forces apprehended Andrews and numerous members of his group. He, along with several comrades, was transported to the Confederate detention center in Chattanooga, Tennessee. After a brief period there, Andrews was relocated to Atlanta, Georgia, where he was incarcerated at the Confederate military prison recognized as Camp Sumter, more commonly known as Andersonville Prison. Andersonville Prison gained infamy for its brutal conditions, severe overcrowding, and alarmingly high death toll among captives. As one of the largest and most infamous prisoner-of-war facilities in the Southern states, the prison was established in February 1864 to house

Union soldiers captured during the conflict.

Andersonville Prison was designed to accommodate a maximum of 10,000 detainees, yet at its zenith, it crammed over 32,000 Union troops into its confines, resulting in severe overcrowding and unhygienic living conditions. Enclosed by a perimeter wall constructed from wooden logs, the prison complex included a narrow stream called Stockade Branch flowing through its center.

Conditions within Andersonville Prison were brutal and appalling. The absence of sufficient shelter, nourishment, and medical assistance led to widespread misery and mortality among the captives. Confederate officials offered scanty rations, primarily comprising cornmeal supplemented occasionally with meager portions of meat or beans. The scarcity of clean water and adequate sanitation facilitated the transmission of diseases like dysentery, scurvy, and typhoid fever.

Prisoners faced extreme temperatures, enduring scorching summers and freezing winters. Overcrowding was rampant, forcing inmates into makeshift shelters or leaving them exposed to the elements.

The Confederate guards at Andersonville were infamous for their cruelty and lack of compassion towards the prisoners' plight. They were known to subject inmates to physical violence, arbitrary killings, and intimidation tactics involving ferocious dogs.

Despite attempts by humanitarian groups and a few Confederate authorities to ease conditions at Andersonville, the mortality rate continued to climb steadily. By the war's end, roughly 13,000 Union soldiers had perished at Andersonville, solidifying its status as one of the most lethal prison camps in U.S. history.

Andrews and several of his Union comrades faced execution by hanging in Atlanta on June 7, 1862, having been tried and found guilty of espionage by the Confederacy. Following the war's end, Captain Henry Wirz, the commandant of Andersonville, was apprehended, tried, and convicted of war crimes related to the mistreatment of prisoners. His execution by hanging occurred in November 1865, marking the sole instance of someone being put to death for war crimes during the Civil War. Today, the Andersonville National Historic Site stands as a tribute to the prisoners who endured and perished within its confines, commemorating their sacrifices and upholding their memory.

Private Jacob Parrott was awarded the Medal of Honor in recognition of the exceptional courage and valor he displayed during the Great Locomotive Chase. Parrott served in the 33rd Ohio Infantry Regiment of the Union Army, which participated in a daring mission orchestrated by civilian scout James J. Andrews deep within Confederate territory in Georgia. Amidst the raid, disguised as civilians, Parrott and his fellow soldiers successfully boarded the General train while it was stationed at the Big Shanty station (now known as Kennesaw, Georgia). Seizing control of the locomotive, they embarked on a northbound journey, systematically sabotaging telegraph lines and railway switches to impede pursuit.

Parrott's contribution was pivotal to the operation, showcasing remarkable bravery and ingenuity during the pursuit. As Confederate troops chased the hijacked train, engaging in intense locomotive races and skirmishes, Parrott and his comrades valiantly defended the General against formidable opposition.

Despite sustaining multiple injuries in the fierce combat, Parrott steadfastly declined to surrender. He persisted in fighting courageously alongside his fellow soldiers until Confederate forces near Ringgold, Georgia, ultimately apprehended them. This occurred after their fuel supply was depleted, compelling them to forsake the General.

Parrott and his fellow raiders were captured and subjected to harsh treatment in several Confederate prison camps. Eventually, he was liberated through a prisoner exchange between Union and Confederate forces and transported to Washington, D.C., where he had the honor of meeting President Abraham Lincoln. Parrott's remarkable bravery and sacrifice during the Great Locomotive Chase earned him the distinction of being the first soldier in American history to receive the Medal of Honor.

His Medal of Honor commended his "exemplary gallantry" and "remarkable bravery" amid daunting challenges, underscoring his extraordinary valor and selflessness throughout the bold and audacious mission. Following the raid, Parrott continued to serve with distinction in the Union Army for the duration of the conflict. He was promoted to second lieutenant in 1863 following the Battle of Stones River and to first lieutenant in 1864. After the war, he returned to Kenton, Ohio, where he pursued his trade as a cabinet maker and operated a stone quarry south of the town.

YOU USED TO BE ABLE TO WIN AN OLYMPIC GOLD MEDAL PLAYING A FLUTE!

The inception of the modern Olympics dates back to 1896, when the inaugural edition of the Olympic Games took place in Athens, Greece. Spearheading this revival was Pierre de Coubertin, a French educator and the visionary behind the establishment of the International Olympic Committee (IOC). Coubertin drew inspiration from the ancient Olympic Games, which had been a prominent fixture in Olympia, Greece, spanning from at least 776 BCE to 393 CE.

The first modern Olympics showcased athletes from 14 nations, engaging in 43 events spanning nine sports. These included athletics, cycling, fencing, gymnastics, swimming, tennis, weightlifting, wrestling, and shooting. The event epitomized international collaboration and athletic prowess, with competitors embodying diverse nationalities and cultural backgrounds.

The triumph of the 1896 Athens Olympics laid the foundation for the modern Olympic movement, dedicated to fostering peace, camaraderie, and cross-cultural exchange through athletic competition. Since its inception, the Olympics have evolved into the premier global sporting event, attracting thousands of athletes from diverse backgrounds to compete across many sports every quadrennial.

The modern Olympics have experienced substantial transformations and growth since their inception, marked by incorporating additional sports, including women's events, and the creation of the Paralympic Games catering to athletes with disabilities. Nevertheless, the fundamental values of the Olympics, centered on integrity, inclusivity, and solidarity, endure, rendering it an emblem of optimism and motivation for individuals globally.

Between 1912 and 1948, the Olympic Games diversified their scope beyond athletic endeavors to encompass competitions in fine arts. This period saw the bestowment of medals for accomplishments in literature, architecture, sculpture, painting, and music. This distinctive facet of the Olympics sought to honor and advance artistic distinction alongside athletic achievement, acknowledging the significance of cultural and intellectual endeavors alongside physical prowess.

The incorporation of artistic competitions into the Olympics drew inspiration from the ancient Greek practice of combining athletic and artistic pursuits in festivals like the ancient Olympic Games. The architects of the modern Olympics aimed to resurrect this comprehensive approach to human accomplishment, contending that the arts were indispensable to fostering the Olympic ethos of promoting unity and eminence.

Contestants in the artistic contests were obligated to present original creations that embodied the Olympic principles of harmony, solidarity, and fair play. Submissions underwent evaluation by expert panels in their respective domains, with medals bestowed upon the foremost achievers, appraised on factors like innovation, technical proficiency, and thematic resonance with the Olympic ethos.

The inclusion of artistic competitions brought a fresh perspective to the Olympic Games, enticing artists globally to exhibit their skills before an international audience. It served as a platform for cultural interchange and creative articulation, nurturing a more profound admiration for the varied artistic heritage of various countries.

Nevertheless, the artistic competitions encountered scrutiny and debate over their alignment with the athletic ethos of the Olympics. Skeptics contended that artistic accomplishments were subjective and posed challenges for impartial evaluation, sparking allegations of prejudice and partiality during the assessment phase.

Consequently, the Olympic authorities opted to cease the artistic competitions following the 1948 London Olympics, focusing solely on athletic contests after that. Although the artistic competitions are no longer featured in the Olympic lineup, they persist as a captivating segment in the Games' narrative, underscoring the convergence of sports and culture and the enduring pursuit of excellence across diverse domains.

The inception of the modern Olympics in Athens signaled the resurgence of the ancient Olympic Games following a hiatus of over 1,500 years. Athens served as the host city for the Olympic Games again in 1906. However, the International Olympic Committee (IOC) did not officially recognize these Games as part of the modern Olympics. Instead, they were held as an interim event bridging the gap between the 1904 and 1908 Summer Olympics. Subsequently, Athens hosted the Summer Olympics for a third time in 2004. This edition of the Games commemorated the 108th anniversary of the modern Olympic movement and marked the long-awaited return of the Olympics to Greece after more than a century.

JOHNNY APPLESEED WAS A REAL PERSON

J ohnny Appleseed, born John Chapman, was an American nurseryman and legendary figure celebrated for his widespread cultivation of apple orchards throughout the American Midwest in the early 19th century. He was born on September 26, 1774, in Leominster, Massachusetts, and dedicated himself to the ambitious endeavor of planting and disseminating apple trees to furnish sustenance, cider, and economic opportunities for pioneers venturing westward.

In the early days of America, apple cider was a popular choice for hydration for various reasons. Firstly, apples were plentiful and thrived in the northeastern United States climate, making cider production abundant and accessible. Additionally, in many areas, cider was a safer option than water due to concerns about water contamination. The fermentation process involved in cider production acted as a natural purifier, eliminating harmful bacteria and pathogens, thus providing a safer alternative to untreated water.

Before widespread refrigeration, preserving perishable food posed a big challenge. Apples, however, presented a solution as they could be stored for extended periods without spoiling, enabling year-round cider production. Furthermore, the fermentation process integral to cider-making served as a natural preservative, effectively extending its shelf life.

The fertile soil and favorable climate of the northeastern United States, especially in New England, facilitated the abundant growth of apple trees. This led to a plentiful supply of affordable apples, ensuring widespread apple cider availability to diverse populations.

Cider-making fostered community bonds, serving as a communal activity that united families and neighborhoods. Typically conducted on small farms and rural settings, it brought people together to press apples and partake in the harvest collectively. Additionally, cider-making became intertwined with social events like harvest festivals and barn raisings, enriching communal gatherings and celebrations.

John Chapman, also known as Johnny Appleseed, journeyed extensively on foot, traversing vast stretches of land in Ohio, Indiana, and Illinois. Along his travels, he frequently established nurseries and left behind saplings of apple trees. Renowned for his peculiar attire, characterized by ragged clothing and a distinctive pot hat, Chapman led a modest and austere lifestyle. He held fervent religious convictions and often imparted his spiritual beliefs to those he met during his nomadic journeys.

Although Johnny Appleseed has ascended to the realm of American folklore, his tale is firmly rooted in historical truth. He played a pivotal role in advancing apple cultivation in the frontier territories of the United States, leaving an enduring imprint through the apple orchards he established. These orchards not only enriched the agricultural landscape but also bolstered the economic growth of the Midwest. His legacy endures as a testament to the pioneering ethos of early America and the importance of environmental conservation.

EATING MUMMIES WAS ONCE CONSIDERED GOOD FOR YOU

Mummies were once hailed as medicine. Particularly during the Renaissance period in Europe, mummies were used for various purposes, including medicinal and artistic ones. It was believed that mummified remains possessed specific therapeutic properties, and they were sometimes ground up and ingested as a remedy for various ailments. Additionally, mummies were sometimes used as a pigment in painting, an ingredient in medicines, or even a curiosity or souvenir.

During the 15th and 16th centuries, spurred partly by the narratives of Crusade travelers, Europeans commenced extensive journeys to Egypt. They became increasingly enamored with Egyptian mummies due to a substance known as medicinal Mumia, which was increasingly acclaimed as a panacea. This burgeoning fascination led to a rise in the plundering of Egyptian tombs and the illicit trade of cadavers in Cairo and Alexandria. In 1424, authorities in Cairo stumbled upon a cache of bodies within the city limits. Upon interrogation, the perpetrators, coerced under pressure, confessed to robbing bodies from nearby tombs, boiling them in water, and gathering the oily residue that surfaced. When probed about their motives, these illicit operators divulged that Europeans would pay twenty-five gold pieces per hundredweight for this eerie substance.

Wealthy and influential Europeans obtained Mumia through reputable merchants in Egypt and the Levant, often acquiring the finished product in Venice. Prominent figures such as King Francis I of France often consistently mixed rhubarb and Mumia with them. Known as "true Mumia," this substance was a dark liquid derived from the preserved remains of ancient Egyptian elites, treated with myrrh, aloes, saffron, and various spices. Extracts from embalmed virgins were considered to have incredibly potent qualities, reflecting an ancient trade that held sway over the medieval Mumia trade.

In the Crusades, Jewish physicians set up a Mumia commerce in the Levant. Their technique involved injecting corpses with low-cost asphalt, followed by wrapping and drying them in the sun. Word of this lucrative trade swiftly spread, leading Egyptians to develop alternative means of acquiring human material. This counterfeit Mumia, sourced from individuals of lower social standing who had been preserved with asphalt, dehydrated travelers, and unlawfully obtained corpses, emerged as the predominant type of Mumia known to most Europeans during the 1500s and 1600s.

In 1586, English explorer John Sanderson ventured into the pyramids to pursue mummified corpses. He described the mummies as having a pitch-like appearance when fractured, and he collected various body parts to study how the flesh had transformed into a substance resembling a drug. Similarly, in 1588, German traveler Samuel Kiechel expressed a desire to explore Egyptian tombs to find mummies, but his local guides discouraged him due to the perceived hazards. Nevertheless, during his stay, Kiechel observed locals scavenging tombs daily, gathering human remains to sell in Cairo markets. He noted that one could purchase an entire individual in Cairo during that time.

Amidst the flourishing trade in Egyptian cadavers, locals began processing and packaging entire embalmed bodies instead of solely extracting the black bituminous substances they yielded. Many of these corpses were sourced from impoverished neighborhoods or remote desert regions where the desiccated remains of lost travelers could be found. Interestingly, some European physicians developed a preference for this particular type of Mumia. Nicasius Le Febre, the chemist of England's King Charles II, asserted that the finest medicinal Mumia originated from "bodies dried up in the hot sands of Libya, where sometimes entire caravans were overwhelmed by sandstorms and suffocated... This sudden suffocation concentrates the spirits in all parts due to the fear and sudden shock experienced by the travelers."

By 1700, Mumia had lost its appeal in Europe. English author John Quincy noted in 1718 that "although Mumia could still be found in medicinal catalogs, it is quite out of use in prescription." In the 1730s, during his travels in the Egyptian deserts, Englishman Richard Pococke witnessed the aftermath of the Mumia craze. He came across numerous skulls strewn across the desert, "many of which probably had been plundered of the bitumen or balsam they contained, when that type of medicine was formerly much more prevalent than it is now."

However, Mumia continued to be supplied by druggists into the 1800s and early 1900s. As late as 1908, the Merck Group in Darmstadt (which remains a pharmaceutical company today) advertised in its catalog: "genuine Egyptian mummy, as long as the supply lasts, 17 marks 50 per kilogram."

SORRY, CHRISTMAS IS CANCELED

O liver Cromwell, an English military and political figure, was instrumental in the English Civil War (1642-1651) and the formation of the Commonwealth of England, a republican regime that supplanted the monarchy. Born in 1599, Cromwell first engaged in farming before venturing into politics. He gained renown for his unwavering Puritan convictions and resistance to King Charles I's initiatives, particularly concerning religious liberties and the monarchy's authority.

During the English Civil War, Cromwell ascended as an adept military strategist and a commander of the Parliamentarian forces, also dubbed the Roundheads, who stood against the Royalists loyal to King Charles I. Cromwell's military triumphs significantly contributed to Parliament's triumph over the Royalists. After the execution of King Charles I in 1649, Cromwell emerged as a pivotal figure in the governance of the Commonwealth of England. He assumed the role of Lord Protector from 1653 until his demise in 1658, effectively governing England as an authoritarian leader. Cromwell's regime was marked by religious intolerance, political suppression, and territorial expansionism.

Oliver Cromwell and the Puritans prohibited Christmas festivities in England during the mid-17th century. They regarded the holiday as a pagan event tainted with unchristian practices, including excessive drinking, feasting, and merrymaking. In those times, Christmas was commemorated much like today, but with heightened zeal, festivities spanning the full 12 days of the holiday. The celebrations included games, exchanges of gifts, social gatherings, and lavish feasts.

Cromwell's administration enacted laws prohibiting the observance of Christmas, and throughout the era of Puritan rule, known as the English Interregnum (1649-1660), Christmas remained unofficially observed. This prohibition was part of a broader campaign to cleanse the Church of England of perceived vestiges of Catholicism and superstition from religious customs. The climax of this effort came with a June 1647 decree aimed at outlawing Christmas and other public holidays. However, this measure proved highly unpopular and even incited riots in some instances. Despite subsequent attempts to enforce the ban on Christmas, they met with significant resistance, leading to a repeal of the legislation in 1660.

THE GUILLOTINE WAS INVENTED TO BE A LESS CRUEL EXECUTION DEVICE

The guillotine, an iconic emblem of the French Revolution, represents a lasting symbol of revolutionary zeal and the quest for fairness. Created by Dr. Joseph-Ignace Guillotin and implemented as a more humane form of capital punishment, its significance is deeply rooted in the chaotic era of late 18th-century France.

Before the guillotine, execution techniques were diverse and frequently led to prolonged agony for those sentenced. Practices such as drawing and quartering were prevalent. The guillotine sought to alleviate this suffering through its rapid and automated precision, offering a swifter and more merciful demise. Its implementation signaled a shift away from the gruesome public executions that were prevalent in France during that era.

The guillotine rose to infamy during the French Revolution, notably throughout the Reign of Terror from 1793 to 1794. Amidst the Revolution's descent into turmoil and bloodshed, thousands, including King Louis XVI and Queen Marie Antoinette, faced their end beneath its blade. Embraced by the revolutionary government, the guillotine emerged as the preferred tool for swiftly and definitively dispatching perceived adversaries of the state. Its adoption as the primary execution method reflected the egalitarian ideals driving the revolutionary fervor in France.

Beyond its association with the French Revolution, the guillotine persisted as a means of execution in France for many years, even after the revolutionary enthusiasm had waned. It remained the sanctioned form of capital punishment until the abolition of the death penalty in France in 1981. Throughout this period, countless individuals, spanning from ordinary citizens to notable figures, met their end by the guillotine, sentenced for offenses ranging from political opposition to everyday crimes.

While often linked with the extremes of the French Revolution, the guillotine also emerged as a symbol of egalitarianism and fairness. Unlike earlier execution techniques, it administered justice uniformly to all condemned individuals, irrespective of their social standing or origins. In principle, it signified a departure from the past's arbitrary and frequently cruel customs, presenting a more standardized and impartial approach to punishment.

The guillotine's impact transcended borders, permeating popular culture and political discussions globally. Its straightforward design and effectiveness rendered it a powerful emblem of state authority, evoking both dread and intrigue among observers. Across literature, art, and cinema, the guillotine has been portrayed as a compelling symbol representing Revolution, justice, and the inherent conflict between individual liberties and societal welfare.

A ROYAL AUDIENCE

In 1710, Native American leaders traveled to Britain to visit Queen Anne. The four Mohawk Kings from one of the Iroquois Confederacy's Five Nations and the Algonquian peoples were highly honored. They were paraded through the streets of London in Royal Carriages and the Queen personally met them at the Court of St. James Palace.

Pocahontas, daughter of Powhatan, the paramount chief of the Powhatan Confederacy in Virginia, embarked on a historic voyage to England in 1616. This journey was orchestrated as a diplomatic endeavor by the Virginia Company of London to bolster relations between the Powhatan Confederacy and the English settlers while showcasing the colony of Virginia.

Pocahontas, known by her given name Matoaka, had forged a special bond with the English settlers in Virginia, notably with Captain John Smith. As documented in Smith's writings, Pocahontas famously intervened to rescue him from capture by her father's warriors in 1607. Whether the incident was embellished or not, it added to Pocahontas's legend and emphasized her role as a mediator between the Native American and English populations in Virginia.

In 1613, English settlers took Pocahontas captive amid the First Anglo-Powhatan War, holding her as a hostage. While in captivity, she embraced Christianity and received the baptismal name "Rebecca." In 1614, she wed John Rolfe, an English colonist, a union that contributed to a period of peace between the English and the Powhatan Confederacy.

Pocahontas' voyage to England in 1616 aimed to highlight the achievements of English colonization in Virginia and portray her as a symbol of unity between the Native American and English settlers. Accompanied by her husband and a modest retinue, Pocahontas reached England in June 1616.

While in England, Pocahontas was showcased to English society as an intriguing novelty and a living example of the potential for harmony between Native Americans and English colonists. She participated in social gatherings, engaged with the English elite, and was granted an audience with King James I and Queen Anne.

Pocahontas' voyage to England sparked significant curiosity and publicity, drawing crowds eager to see the "Indian princess" from the New World. Yet, amidst the attention, she faced personal trials, contending with illness and longing for her homeland.

Unfortunately, Pocahontas fell ill during her time in England and passed away in March 1617 at approximately 21 years old. She was laid to rest in Gravesend, Kent, where she had been residing before her intended voyage back to Virginia. Although her life was cut short, Pocahontas' visit to England is a notable episode in the narrative of early English settlement in North America and the intricate interplay between Native American and European societies.

In the early 18th century, diplomatic exchanges between European and Native American nations were characterized by diplomacy, negotiation, and mutual interest. A noteworthy element of this diplomacy was the journeys undertaken by Native American leaders to European capitals, such as London. Among these visits, those that took place during the rule of Queen Anne of Great Britain are particularly noteworthy in the annals of Native American-European interactions.

Queen Anne assumed the British throne in 1702 amid European colonial expansion and strife in North America. In this context, Native American leaders aimed to navigate the intricacies of European politics and establish alliances advantageous to their tribes. Visits to London allowed these leaders to interact directly with British authorities and advocate for their interests on a global platform.

An exceptional instance of such diplomatic encounters unfolded in 1710, as a group of Native American dignitaries from the Iroquois Confederacy embarked on a journey to London to confer with Queen Anne. Guided by Hendrick Peters, a prominent Mohawk chief, the delegation aimed to enlist British assistance in their ongoing struggles against rival Native American factions and French colonial interests. The outcome of this visit was the formalization of a treaty between the Iroquois Confederacy and the British Crown, solidifying an alliance that persisted for generations.

The journeys undertaken by Native American leaders to Britain during Queen Anne's rule carried profound consequences for both indigenous tribes and European colonial powers. For Native Americans, these visits represented a chance to affirm their autonomy and bargain for advantageous terms with European nations. Through direct interactions with European monarchs and authorities, Native American leaders aimed to safeguard their territories, establish beneficial trade pacts, and navigate the intricate webs of European colonial diplomacy.

These visits provided European colonial powers with valuable insights into the intricate workings of Native American diplomacy. They presented an occasion to forge alliances that could advance their strategic objectives in North America by cultivating relationships with Native American tribes. European powers aimed to access the profitable fur trade and form military partnerships to counteract competing colonial forces.

The visits undertaken by Native American leaders to Britain during Queen Anne's reign stand as an intriguing episode in the annals of Native American-European interactions. These diplomatic engagements underscored the agency and diplomatic understanding of Native American leaders, who adeptly maneuvered within the intricate web of European colonial politics to safeguard the interests of their tribes. While the consequences of these visits were complex and varied, they undeniably wielded considerable influence in shaping the trajectory of colonial history in North America.

DID THOMAS EDISON "INVENT" HOLLYWOOD?

Thomas Edison did not develop every invention he patented on his own. Although renowned as a remarkably productive inventor with more than a thousand patents to his name across diverse innovations, he also relied on teams of engineers, scientists, and technicians at his laboratories, notably the renowned Menlo Park facility in New Jersey. Through collaborative efforts on numerous projects, these teams brought their expertise and ingenuity to Edison's inventive endeavors.

Edison's reputation rested not only on his inventive prowess but also on his adeptness as an entrepreneur, his capacity to transform inventions into commercial ventures, and his skillful marketing and promotional tactics. However, there were instances where he claimed credit for inventions from his laboratories, sparking debates and discontent, especially among those who believed that his collaborators warranted greater acknowledgment for their creative inputs.

An illustrative instance is the creation of the electric light bulb. Although Edison is often attributed with its invention, it was a product of progressive enhancements built on earlier concepts by multiple inventors. Several innovators, such as Humphry Davy, Warren de la Rue, and Joseph Swan, explored electric lighting before Edison's endeavors. Nonetheless, their designs either proved impractical for broad application or needed more longevity for commercial viability.

In 1879, Edison achieved a breakthrough with his team at Menlo Park, New Jersey, by creating a filament crafted from carbonized bamboo, boasting a lifespan of more than 1200 hours. This marked a substantial advancement over prior filaments, which tended to expire after just a few hours. Moreover, Edison devised a vacuum pump to extract air from the bulb, thereby staving off filament oxidation and premature burnout.

Edison's light bulb became the inaugural model to undergo mass production and be made available to the general public, initiating the era of widespread electric lighting. While he didn't invent the light bulb, his advancements rendered electric lighting feasible and convenient for ordinary usage, leading to his recognition as the "inventor" of the light bulb.

During the late 19th and early 20th centuries, Thomas Edison had many pivotal patents pertaining to motion picture technology, including the Kinetoscope, a precursor to modern film projectors. Edison vigorously defended these patents and actively pursued legal recourse against anyone found to be infringing upon them. Consequently, a hostile environment emerged for filmmakers operating in the New York area, where Edison's Motion Picture Patents Company (MPPC), colloquially known as the "Edison Trust," wielded significant influence over the industry. To evade potential legal entanglements and preserve creative autonomy, filmmakers sought refuge in locales beyond the jurisdiction of Edison's patents. Los Angeles emerged as an appealing destination due to several factors. Its distance from New York complicated the enforcement of Edison's patents by his agents, rendering it a more conducive environment for filmmakers seeking to avoid patent-related constraints.

Freed from the constraining grip of the Edison Trust, filmmakers in Los Angeles found themselves liberated to explore novel techniques and narrative approaches, sparking a period characterized by swift innovation and artistic maturation during the silent film era. This unfettered creative expression was the bedrock for Hollywood's eventual emergence as the preeminent global entertainment hub.

Although Thomas Edison is often credited with inventing the light bulb, the reality is that he made significant improvements to earlier designs and played a crucial role in creating the first commercially viable incandescent light bulb.

THE VIKINGS WERE THE FIRST NON-INDIGENOUS PEOPLE TO DISCOVER AMERICA

Many historians believe that the Vikings reached the shores of North America around 1000 AD, well before Christopher Columbus' famous voyage in 1492. The leader of this expedition was a Norse explorer named Leif Erikson. He was born around 970 A.D. in Iceland, and his father was Erik the Red, a renowned Norse explorer responsible for establishing the first Norse settlement in Greenland.

Historical records suggest that Leif Erikson and his crew reached the shores of present-day Newfoundland, Canada, where they established a settlement known as Vinland, likely in the area now identified as L'Anse aux Meadows. The precise date of the Viking discovery of North America remains uncertain but is generally thought to have occurred in the early 11th century. Accounts in Norse sagas, which are written narratives of Viking history and exploration, offer some of the earliest documentation of the Viking presence in North America. These sagas recount Leif Erikson's journey to Vinland and the interactions between Norse settlers and the indigenous inhabitants they encountered.

The Viking exploration of North America is unparalleled in the history of exploration and intercultural interactions. It is a testament to the Vikings' exceptional seamanship and their fearlessness in expeditions to unexplored territories to discover new lands and resources. Although their occupation of North America was brief and limited, its impact on the region's history and cultural heritage is significant and long-lasting.

Leif Erikson had a lasting impact on his heritage and North American society. His remarkable achievements in exploration and pioneering spirit have made him a revered figure whose legacy is celebrated through various means such as statues, monuments, and the observance of Leif Erikson Day on October 9th in the United States and other parts of the world. His contributions have cemented his place in history as a symbol of bravery, determination, and cultural exchange.

LONG IN THE TOOTH?

Humans have been performing dentistry for thousands of years, as evidenced by historical records from ancient civilizations like the Egyptians, Greeks, and Romans. Although primitive by today's standards, dental care in ancient times was vital in managing oral health and relieving discomfort.

During ancient times in Egypt, dental care was administered by specialized professionals referred to as "dentists." These early practitioners possessed expertise in addressing various dental conditions like toothaches, cavities, and gum disease. Employing basic instruments like hand drills, forceps, and abrasive powders, they used procedures to clean and extract teeth.

Likewise, in ancient Greek and Roman civilizations, individuals practiced dentistry and devised methods for filling cavities using lead and bronze. They also developed techniques for tooth extraction and cleaning.

During the Middle Ages, extending into the Renaissance era, dentistry progressed, albeit gradually. Dentists in Europe during this period predominantly concentrated on tooth removal and alleviating dental discomfort rather than emphasizing preventative measures.

In the 18th and 19th centuries, dentistry started to take shape as the profession we are familiar with today. Advancements such as the creation of modern dental tools, the founding of dental education institutions, and the introduction of anesthesia transformed the dental field, enabling more sophisticated treatments and procedures.

The initial braces, crafted from metal, emerged in the 18th century. French dentist Pierre Fauchard is commonly attributed with pioneering these early braces circa 1728. Fauchard's design featured flat metal strips positioned atop the teeth and linked with thread or wire.

Nonetheless, braces didn't have increased usage and effectiveness until the 19th century. During the early 1800s, another French dentist named Christophe-François Delabarre introduced the wire crib, which encircled the teeth and applied pressure to align them.

During the late 19th and early 20th centuries, progress in orthodontic methods and materials continued to enhance the efficiency of braces. Edward Angle, an American dentist commonly hailed as the "father of modern orthodontics," played a pivotal role in this advancement. Angle revolutionized orthodontics by standardizing the application of braces and introducing techniques like brackets and wires to correct tooth alignment gradually.

Over the 20th century, braces underwent continual

refinement with materials, methodologies, and aesthetic advancements. While conventional metal braces retained their popularity, alternatives like ceramic braces and clear aligners emerged, providing patients with more inconspicuous options for orthodontic correction.

In general, although the modalities and strategies within dentistry have undergone a substantial transformation over the years, humans have engaged in some manner of dental care for millennia, acknowledging the crucial role of oral health in overall wellness.

ANTHONY COMSTOCK TRIED TO GET A PICTURE OF A BALLERINA BANNED BECAUSE HE THOUGHT IT WAS "LEWD"

Anthony Comstock was a prominent figure in American history who was crucial in enforcing moral values and obscenity laws during the late 19th and early 20th centuries. His actions had a significant impact on the legislation regarding censorship, obscenity, reproductive rights, and public discourse.

Comstock was born in New Canaan, Connecticut, on March 7, 1844. He grew up in a very religious household. His parents' devout Christian beliefs heavily influenced him and his later work as an adult. He served in the Union Army during the Civil War, and while enlisted, his moral convictions were strengthened; he dedicated his life to what he believed was good behavior.

1872 Anthony Comstock co-founded the New York Society for the Suppression of Vice (NYSSV). This organization was dedicated to the noble cause of combating obscenity, vice, and immorality in society. As the secretary of the NYSSV, Comstock wielded significant influence in advocating for stricter laws and regulations that he believed would help society preserve its moral values and protect its citizens from the harmful effects of obscenity.

Comstock attacked literature, art, and other media that he considered immoral or disgusting as part of his campaign against obscenity. He advocated for the enactment of regulations like the Comstock Act of 1873, which made it illegal to send pornographic publications via mail in the United States. Comstock also worked to hide information about reproductive health and birth control. He spent a great deal of effort limiting access to contraceptive knowledge and devices because he believed that contraception was evil.

Anthony Comstock was an American moral crusader who dedicated his life to upholding ethical standards by combating obscenity and vice. His zealous campaign against obscenity and birth control had an immense impact on American society, shaping public discourse and legislation on issues related to censorship, obscenity, and reproductive rights. However, his methods and tactics were often criticized for their infringement on civil liberties and freedom of expression, causing a complex legacy. While some praise his efforts to uphold moral standards, others condemn his authoritarian approach to social reform. Nevertheless, Comstock's influence on American society cannot be understated, and his actions have had enduring effects that continue to shape modern-day conversations on censorship and freedom of expression.

Comstockery refers to a type of censorship based on moralistic principles that involve strict adherence to the values of the Victorian era. It is characterized by suppressing anything considered offensive to public decency or morality. The term is often used to criticize excessive efforts to limit freedom of expression and speech in the name of upholding moral standards.

KNOCKER UPPERS
WERE THE FIRST
ALARM CLOCKS

D uring the Industrial Revolution in Britain and Ireland, timekeeping was needed as society shifted from agriculture to mass-scale factory work.

As urbanization increased, people relied on "knocker uppers" or "knockers up" to wake them up, as they could no longer rely on the crowing of roosters or the ringing of church bells. These knocker-uppers were human alarm clocks that used fishing rod-like sticks, soft hammers, rattles, and peashooters to rouse the sleeping by tapping on their windows.

The Great Britain Industrial Revolution was the center of a significant shift from rural and agricultural societies to urbanized industrial centers. The development of important innovations such as the steam engine, mechanized textile production, and the establishment of iron and coal industries led Britain into a new era of manufacturing and commerce. This transformation led to the emergence of cities like Manchester, Birmingham, and Sheffield as hubs of industrial activity, attracting workers from rural areas in search of employment opportunities. In contrast, Ireland's experience with the Industrial Revolution was more complicated, influenced by its colonial history and rural economy.

While some parts of the country, particularly in the north, embraced industrialization and experienced the growth of linen, shipbuilding, and brewing industries, most of rural Ireland remained unaffected by the industrial advancements seen in Britain. Instead, most of Ireland's population relied heavily on agriculture, engaging in small-scale farming or tenant labor on large estates. The Industrial Revolution had significant social implications for both Ireland and Great Britain. Urbanization led to overcrowded and unsanitary living conditions in industrial cities, resulting in widespread poverty, disease, and social unrest. The rise of factory-based production disrupted traditional work and family life modes, as men, women, and children found themselves working long hours in factories for meager wages.

Moreover, the Industrial Revolution in Ireland intersected with broader political and social issues, including the struggle for independence and the impact of British colonial policies on Irish society. The Great Famine of the 1840s, worsened by Ireland's dependence on agriculture and the export of food to Britain, further compounded the challenges faced by the Irish population during this tumultuous period.

The job of a knocker upper was to walk through the streets or alleys near industrial areas and wake workers from their sleep. They used long sticks or poles to tap on the windows of workers' homes. Some knocker uppers gently tapped the windows using pea shooters or small rocks, while others used more creative methods like singing or shouting. The primary purpose of this occupation was to ensure that workers arrived on time for their shifts, as being late could lead to fines or even job termination.

"Hard Times" is a novel by Charles Dickens that offers a glimpse into the lives of factory workers in England during the Industrial Revolution. Although the book focuses on the harsh realities workers face in factories, it also mentions characters who perform tasks like knocker-uppers, ensuring that workers wake up on time for their shifts.

The practice of using knocker-uppers continued until the 1970s, before the advent of alarm clocks and smartphone alarms.

During the height of the Industrial Revolution, knocker uppers were essential for maintaining workers' productivity in urban areas. However, this occupation gradually faded as alarm clocks and other timekeeping devices became widely available.

"UNDER GOD" WAS ADDED TO THE PLEDGE OF ALLEGIANCE TO STICK IT TO THE RUSSIANS

T he Pledge of Allegiance promises loyalty to the United States and is often recited by citizens during public events and gatherings.

The Pledge of Allegiance was first written in 1885 by Captain George Thatcher Balch, a Union Army officer in the Civil War. He later wrote a book on teaching patriotism to children in public schools. The original version had a different text than the one used at present. The current Pledge of Allegiance has its roots in the late 19th century and is credited to Francis Bellamy, a Christian Socialist minister. In 1892, Bellamy revised Balch's verse as part of a magazine promotion surrounding the World's Columbian Exposition, which celebrated the 400th anniversary of

Christopher Columbus' arrival in the Americas.

In 1892, Francis Bellamy created the original version of the Pledge of Allegiance to promote national unity and patriotism among schoolchildren. The Pledge went like this: "I pledge allegiance to my Flag and the Republic for which it stands, one nation, indivisible, with liberty and justice for all." The Pledge became popular quickly when the magazine sent leaflets containing part of Bellamy's Pledge to schools nationwide. On October 21, 1892, over 10,000 children recited the verse together. As time went on, the Pledge of Allegiance was adopted by schools and civic organizations throughout the country to show loyalty and respect for the United States.

Bellamy's version of the Pledge, essentially the same as the one officially adopted by Congress 50 years later in 1942, was given its official name, The Pledge of Allegiance, in 1945. In 1951, the Knights of Columbus, the world's largest Catholic fraternal service organization, began including "under God" in the Pledge of Allegiance. In 1953, at the suggestion of a correspondent, Representative Louis C. Rabaut (D-Mich.) sponsored a resolution to add the words "under God" to the Pledge. The phrase "under God" was then incorporated into the Pledge of Allegiance on June 14, 1954, by a Joint Resolution of Congress. The phrase "under God" was added to the Pledge of Allegiance during the Cold War to emphasize America's religious heritage and to counter communism and atheism.

The Cold War lasted from the late 1940s to the early 1990s. It was a period of intense rivalry between the United States and the Soviet Union, marked by tensions, competition, and the threat of nuclear conflict. Although the primary drivers of the Cold War were differences in political and economic ideologies - capitalism and communism, religion also played a significant role in shaping perceptions and narratives on both sides.

Religion, especially Christianity, was often used as a significant part of American identity and a defense against the perceived atheistic and godless ideology of communism. American political leaders, such as President Dwight D. Eisenhower, presented the Cold War as a contest between the powers of democracy, freedom, and Judeo-Christian values represented by the United States and the atheistic, godless ideology of communism represented by the Soviet Union.

During the Cold War, religion was crucial in shaping propaganda and rhetoric. American politicians and media often depicted communism as being fundamentally opposed to religion and hostile to religious freedom. Meanwhile, Soviet leaders aimed to portray communism as a progressive ideology that would free people from the chains of religious superstition and exploitation.

During the Cold War, religion was manipulated to advance the interests of the United States and the Soviet Union in proxy wars. This was especially evident in regions with religious significance, like the Middle East. The two superpowers supported and opposed governments and movements based on their perceived alignment with their ideologies and interests. This often worsened existing religious conflicts and tensions.

During the Cold War, which was mainly a geopolitical and ideological conflict, religion was crucial in influencing perceptions, propaganda, and policies. The era witnessed the merging of religion with politics, nationalism, and ideology, revealing the intricate connection between religious beliefs and the pursuit of power and influence on the global stage.

During the Cold War in 1954, the phrase "under God" was added to the Pledge of Allegiance to differentiate the United States as a nation founded on religious beliefs and principles. In 1956, "In God We Trust" became the official motto of the United States, replacing the previous slogan "E Pluribus Unum" (Out of Many, One). This change further emphasized the religious foundations of American identity in contrast to the atheistic ideology of communism.

The Pledge of Allegiance has been a topic of controversy and debate. Some critics argue that including "under God" goes against the principle of separation of church and state stated in the Constitution's First Amendment. Others raise concerns about the mandatory recitation of the Pledge in schools, citing issues related to freedom of speech and individual autonomy.

THE HOLLYWOOD
FOOTPRINT FIASCO

Showman Sid Grauman and partners Douglas Fairbanks and Mary Pickford commissioned the theater. Architect Raymond M. Kennedy was tasked with its design, and it officially opened on May 18, 1927. Modeled after ancient Chinese architecture, the theater boasts intricate embellishments, pagodas, and a majestic courtyard adorned with a mural depicting a dragon.

Born Gladys Louise Smith on April 8, 1892, in Toronto, Canada, Mary Pickford was a trailblazing actress, producer, and co-founder of United Artists. Renowned as one of the most influential personalities in the nascent film industry, she ascended to cultural icon status during the silent film era.

Pickford initiated her acting journey in the theater during childhood, touring with her family's traveling theater ensemble. Her film debut came in 1909 with "The Violin Maker of Cremona," marking the beginning of her rapid ascent to stardom, propelled by her remarkable talent and on-screen charisma.

During the 1910s and 1920s, Pickford earned the moniker "America's Sweetheart" and emerged as one of Hollywood's most beloved and well-compensated actresses. She headlined many triumphant silent films, frequently embodying innocent, youthful personas that deeply connected with viewers.

Among Pickford's standout works are "Tess of the Storm Country" (1914), "Poor Little Rich Girl" (1917), "Stella Maris" (1918), and "Little Lord Fauntleroy" (1921). Renowned for their emotional resonance and authenticity, her performances garnered critical praise and endeared her to audiences.

Apart from her acting pursuits, Pickford displayed astute business acumen, pioneering profit-sharing agreements with film studios, marking one of the earliest instances of such negotiations by actors. In 1919, she established United Artists alongside Charlie Chaplin, D.W. Griffith, and her spouse, Douglas Fairbanks, which granted them substantial autonomy over their cinematic endeavors and professional trajectories. Pickford's illustrious career earned her numerous accolades, including an Academy Award for Best Actress for her role in "Coquette" (1929), a historic achievement as the first Canadian recipient of an Oscar. Furthermore, she was honored with an honorary Academy Award in 1976 for her profound contributions to the film industry.

The Chinese Theatre is renowned for its forecourt, boasting nearly 200 celebrity handprints, footprints, and autographs embedded in the concrete pavement. This tradition originated when actress Norma Talmadge inadvertently stepped into wet cement during the theater's construction, sparking the custom of immortalizing stars' imprints.

Norma Talmadge, an acclaimed American silent film actress, was among the leading luminaries of the silent era. Born on May 26, 1894, in Jersey City, New Jersey, Talmadge embarked on her acting journey in the early 1910s, sharing the screen in silent films alongside her sisters, Constance and Natalie Talmadge.

Talmadge earned widespread acclaim for her roles in dramatic films, frequently depicting empathetic heroines in romantic dramas. Renowned for her expressive acting prowess, she had a remarkable knack for conveying emotions solely through her performances, showcasing her talent in silent cinema.

Throughout the 1910s and 1920s, Talmadge headlined numerous successful films for various studios, including Vitagraph Studios and First National Pictures. Among her notable works are "The Battle Cry of Peace" (1915), "The Ghosts of Yesterday" (1918), and "Smilin' Through" (1922). Experiencing the pinnacle of her fame in the mid-1920s, she ranked among Hollywood's highest-paid actresses of that era, boasting a sizable fan base drawn to her glamorous on-screen presence. However, with the advent of sound in the late 1920s, Talmadge encountered challenges in transitioning to "talkies," leading to a decline in her career. She ultimately retired from acting in 1930.

The Chinese Theatre, situated in the heart of Hollywood, has played host to numerous movie premieres for decades. Legendary films such as "The Wizard of Oz" and "Star Wars" have been premiered here, cementing its status as a Hollywood icon and a must-visit destination for tourists from all over the world.

In 2013, the Chinese electronics company TCL Corporation collaborated with the theater, resulting in a name change to TCL Chinese Theatre. However, this change has not affected its appeal as a popular venue for movie premieres, special events, and guided tours. The TCL Chinese Theatre continues to be a beloved landmark and a treasured part of Hollywood's cultural heritage.

JOUSTING IS THE
OFFICIAL SPORT
OF MARYLAND

T he roots of jousting lie in medieval Europe, where it gained prominence as a favored combat and entertainment spectacle among knights during the Middle Ages. Although somewhat ambiguous, its origins can be traced back to the 11th century. Jousting likely developed from earlier manifestations of cavalry combat and tournaments conducted as integral components of military training regimens.

During the High Middle Ages (11th to 13th centuries), jousting became a pivotal component of European knightly tournaments. These tournaments, characterized by their elaborate nature, served as platforms to demonstrate knights' martial prowess, equestrian abilities, and chivalric ideals. Often organized to commemorate significant events such as weddings, coronations, or religious festivities, these tournaments drew participants and spectators from diverse strata of society.

In the customary jousting tournament, two knights would

gallop towards each other astride their horses, wielding lances to strike their opponent's shield or armor to dismount them. Points were granted depending on the precision and impact of the lance strikes, with the victor often receiving prizes or commendations.

Jousting underwent evolutionary changes, leading to the emergence of diverse rules, formats, and competition styles across different European regions; alongside the classic joust, tournaments diversified to encompass alternative combat forms like melee combat (sword fighting), mounted combat using blunted weapons or contests of equestrian skill.

Throughout the Late Middle Ages and into the Renaissance era, jousting retained its appeal among the nobility, yet its importance dwindled gradually due to shifts in warfare and societal norms that made the knightly code of chivalry obsolete. By the 17th century, jousting had primarily lost its prominence as a competitive sport, although remnants of its practice persisted in ceremonial or symbolic contexts.

In contemporary times, jousting has seen a resurgence in fascination as a historical reenactment, serving as entertainment at Renaissance fairs and medieval festivals and evolving into a competitive sport in its own regard. Presently, organized jousting tournaments and associations are dedicated to upholding the customs and skills of medieval jousting, guaranteeing that this ancient pursuit remains captivating for individuals worldwide.

Jousting is distinct in Maryland's cultural heritage and is acknowledged as the official state sport. Maryland's association with jousting traces back to the colonial period, introduced by English settlers. The sport became deeply rooted in Maryland's rural areas and frequently featured at community gatherings such as local fairs, festivals, and tournaments.

During the 19th and early 20th centuries, jousting retained popularity as a favored pastime in Maryland, attracting participants and onlookers from all corners of the state to competitive gatherings. These jousting tournaments evolved into beloved traditions within numerous rural communities, doubling as social occasions and tributes to Maryland's rich equestrian legacy.

In the present day, although jousting may not be as prevalent as in earlier times, it maintains a unique importance in Maryland. The state remains an active host of jousting tournaments and competitions, especially during the summer, coinciding with county fairs and festivals. These gatherings draw individuals of various ages, from seasoned practitioners to novices keen on embracing the excitement of the sport.

Moreover, Maryland is the birthplace of modern organized jousting competitions. Established in 1950, the Maryland Jousting Tournament Association is one of the United States' oldest and most vibrant jousting organizations. Through its array of organized events, educational initiatives, and outreach endeavors, the association fervently promotes the sport, guaranteeing that jousting remains an enduring element of Maryland's cultural legacy for future generations.

BUBBLE, BUBBLE, TOIL AND... FLOWERS?

E ye of newt, toe of frog, and wool of bat are old terms for mustard seed, buttercup, and holly leaves.

In William Shakespeare's "Macbeth," three witches, referred to as the "Weird Sisters" or the "Three Witches," hold a central position in the progression of the tragic narrative. These enigmatic and otherworldly entities exert substantial sway over the decisions and destinies of the characters.

They stand over a cauldron making potions and singing the following verse:

"Fillet of a fenny snake, In the cauldron boil and bake; Eye of newt and toe of frog, Wool of bat and tongue of dog, Adder's fork and blind-worm's sting, Lizard's leg and owlet's wing, For a charm of powerful trouble, Like a hell-broth boil and bubble."

Nonetheless, the elements utilized in their potion weren't literal frog eyeballs but herbs and plants referred to by colloquial names prevalent during Shakespeare's era. "Eye of newt," "toe of frog," and "wool of bat" are antiquated terms for mustard seed, buttercup, and holly leaves, respectively.

Here are some other "odd" names for common plants:

Toe of frog = Buttercup

Tongue of dog = Gypsyflower

Adders fork = Least Adder's-tongue, a type of fern

Wool of bat = Holly Leaves

Physically, the witches are portrayed as grotesque and unsettling beings, often characterized by their beards, weather-beaten skin, and unkempt hair, contributing to their unearthly demeanor. Their presence instills a sense of dread and apprehension, establishing the dark and ominous ambiance of the play.

In the play "Macbeth," the witches are not bystanders but participants in the story's events. They appear in the opening scene amid thunder and lightning, hinting at the turmoil and havoc they will incite. Throughout the play, they involve themselves in prophecy and manipulation, tempting Macbeth with promises of authority and renown.

The witches' predictions trigger Macbeth's ambition and his descent into tyranny. Foretelling Macbeth's rise to Thane of Cawdor and eventual kingship of Scotland, these prophecies sow the seeds of his ambition and spark his ruthless pursuit of power. Despite their deceitful nature, the witches' predictions ultimately materialize, propelling Macbeth towards murder and tyranny in his quest for the throne.

Beyond their prophetic abilities, the witches possess supernatural powers that enable them to cast spells and manipulate reality. They exhibit the capability to vanish and reappear at will, along with influencing the weather and controlling natural elements. These powers deepen their mystique and reinforce their role as agents of chaos and disruption.

In "Macbeth," the witches represent the darker forces in the world and symbolize themes such as ambition, fate, and the repercussions of unbridled desire. Their presence underscores the play's exploration of the conflict between fate and free will and the corruptive nature of power, adding depth to its moral and thematic complexity.

William Shakespeare composed "Macbeth" between 1603 and 1607, but the exact date of its creation remains uncertain. It likely occurred during the reign of King James I of England, who assumed the throne in 1603.

Various factors, including the Gunpowder Plot of 1605, might have influenced Shakespeare's choice to write "Macbeth" during this period. This conspiracy, orchestrated by Catholic insurgents aiming to assassinate King James and topple the Protestant regime, was uncovered and thwarted, leading to the execution of the perpetrators and heightening concerns about political instability and threats to the monarchy.

Moreover, King James I harbored a deep interest in witchcraft and the supernatural, a fascination mirrored in "Macbeth" through the witches' prominent role and the exploration of themes such as fate, prophecy, and the occult. Shakespeare may have leveraged King James's intrigue in these topics to engage his royal patron and audience.

"Macbeth" is a masterpiece that takes us on a journey of power, guilt, and ambition. Shakespeare's timeless play explores the corrupting influence of unrestrained ambition and how it often leads to downfall. It's a story that continues to captivate audiences and leaves them questioning the extent to which we can all succumb to our darkest desires. These enduring themes would have resonated with Shakespeare's contemporary audience and continue to captivate modern audiences, cementing "Macbeth" as one of Shakespeare's most enduring and extensively analyzed works.

WHERE'S YOUR POTATO SACK?

In 1907, a woman was arrested on a beach in Boston for wearing a one-piece swimsuit

During the late 1800s to the early 1900s, women's bathing suits, also known as "swimming costumes," were remarkably cumbersome. These garments were long, covering most body parts, designed to be non-transparent, and even incorporated weights on the skirts to prevent them from floating in the water. In the early 1900s, women ventured into the water clad in black, knee-length dresses with puffed sleeves made of wool, worn over bloomers, long black stockings, bathing slippers, and ribboned swim caps.

Annette Kellerman, an Australian native, rose to prominence in the United States as a professional swimmer and performer. By 1905, she held all the world records for women's swimming. Renowned as a vaudeville sensation, her act featured daring high dives and mesmerizing underwater ballet. Newspapers hailed her as "The Original Mermaid."

Kellerman sparked controversy when she opted for a daring one-piece, form-fitting bodysuit, leading to her arrest on a Boston beach in 1907. She trained at Revere Beach to prepare for a 13-mile swim meet in Boston. However, her attire, featuring a one-piece bathing suit with shorts ending above the knees, shocked bystanders, prompting the intervention of law enforcement and resulting in her apprehension on charges of indecency.

Following her arrest, Kellerman modified her swimsuit to comply with regulations, adding arm coverage and extending the leg coverage. This adaptation allowed her to skirt the laws and evade further arrests. As an athlete and swimmer, the conventional swimwear of the era proved impractical for Kellerman, who frequently performed in public tanks.

Reflecting on the 1907 incident in a 1953 interview with the Boston Sunday Globe, Kellerman reflected on the arrest. She remembered being shocked. Her father was shocked too because she was a "good girl." However, the judge was lenient, and he allowed Kellerman to wear a long cape over her swimsuit until she got to the water's edge.

The Globe article highlighted Kellerman's remarkable achievements, emphasizing her groundbreaking feats that shook the competitive swimming community. In 1905, she swam across three-quarters of the English Channel, setting a record with her 10-and-a-half-hour effort and capturing global attention. The article noted her world records, including the 100-yard dash, and highlighted two enduring achievements: the 26-mile swim from Dover to Ramsgate in 1908 and an underwater time of 3 minutes and 27 seconds.

Kellerman's swimming career persisted, culminating in creating a synchronized swim show featured in the 1952 film "Million Dollar Mermaid" alongside Esther Williams. She eventually settled in California and later earned a Hollywood Walk of Fame star. This solidified her legacy in the entertainment capital.

TULIP BULBS WERE ONCE MORE VALUABLE THAN GOLD IN HOLLAND

During the 17th Century Dutch Republic, tulips, in particular, gained notoriety amid the phenomenon known as 'tulip mania,' where speculators traded the flower's bulbs for exorbitant sums until the market spectacularly collapsed. Originating from the Pamir and Tien Shan mountain ranges in central Asia, tulips were exotic newcomers to Western Europe, coveted for their rarity and allure.

Each year, certain bulbs underwent a phenomenon known as 'breaking,' transforming from single-colored blooms to intricate patterns involving multiple hues. Unbeknownst at the time, this striated effect was caused by a virus, yet diseased tulips with distinct patterns became highly sought after in the Dutch Republic. Botanists competed to breed captivating hybrid varieties called 'cultivars.'

In the early 17th Century, a network of scholars emerged, exchanging local and international tulip cultivars. As this network expanded, trading evolved from a friendly exchange to a commercial venture, with scholars accommodating requests from unfamiliar parties, eventually leading to transactions for profit.

Tulip mania coincided with a prosperous period for the United Provinces, which dominated global trade and emerged as the wealthiest nation in Europe. Consequently, aristocrats, merchants, and even middle-class artisans had disposable income to invest in luxuries like expensive flowers.

Demand for tulips soared, with prices skyrocketing as tales of unprecedented profits circulated. Speculators flocked to the market, driving prices to dizzying heights. By 1637, a single bulb of the coveted Semper Augustus variety was valued at an astonishing 10,000 guilders.

The winter of 1636-37 marked the peak of tulip mania, with frenzied trading occurring among people from various walks of life in smoky tavern backrooms. However, the market abruptly collapsed in early February 1637, as most speculators could no longer afford even the cheapest bulbs, leading to a dramatic decline in demand and values.

Remarkably, despite the financial turmoil caused by tulip mania, the Dutch maintained their appreciation for flowers in art. Dutch flower painting endured for centuries, although there is a noticeable absence of flower paintings from the 1630s, suggesting a temporary aversion to floral imagery following the trauma of

tulip mania.

THE FIRST PERSON CROSSED NIAGARA FALLS BY TIGHTROPE IN 1859

I n the winter of 1858, Jean François Gravelet, a 34-year-old French acrobat widely known as Monsieur Charles Blondin, embarked on a daring venture to Niagara Falls with the ambitious goal of becoming the first person to traverse the treacherous "boiling cataract" on a tightrope. With the icy banks and tumultuous winds surrounding the gorge, Blondin wisely postponed the spectacle until more favorable weather conditions prevailed. Unlike contemporary performers, he eschewed safety measures such as nets, believing that anticipating mishaps only increased their likelihood. His tightrope, spanning 1,300 feet long and crafted from two-inch-thick hemp, would be his only safeguard against the churning waters below.

Blondin, born in 1824, was a diminutive figure, standing at only five feet five inches and weighing 140 pounds. Sporting bright blue eyes and golden hair, which earned him his moniker, he held firm to the belief that a tightrope walker was innately gifted, akin to a poet, rather than crafted through training. His affinity for the art manifested at the tender age of four when he ascended a rope between two chairs placed a short distance apart. By age five, he was enrolled at the École de Gymnase in Lyon. Blondin's journey to America commenced in 1855 under the auspices of theatrical agent William Niblo. Initially slated to perform with Franconi's Equestrian Troop, he conceived the audacious idea of traversing Niagara Falls. Described by his manager, Harry Colcord, as more of a fantastical sprite than a mere mortal, Blondin's remarkable abilities on the tightrope were likened to those of a mythical being. Colcord mused that had Blondin lived in an earlier era, he would have been regarded as possessed by a devil. He marveled at Blondin's ability to glide along the rope with the ease of a bird in flight.

Blondin was acutely aware of the public's fascination with the macabre and embraced the spectacle of onlookers wagering on the likelihood of his demise in the swirling waters below. (The prevailing sentiment among most bettors was grim.) On the fateful morning of June 30, 1859, approximately 25,000 thrill-seekers descended upon Niagara Falls via train and steamer, dispersing across either the American or Canadian side in search of prime viewing spots. The Canadian vantage point was reputed to offer a better view. Both riverbanks were full of spectators, including politicians, judges, clergy, military leaders, members of Congress, wealthy financiers, artists, newspaper editors, academics, debutantes, sales clerks, and peddlers. Amidst the crowds, vendors plied their wares, hawking everything from lemonade to whiskey, while Colcord led guided tours for the press, elucidating the intricacies of Blondin's impending feat.

A slender rope, barely exceeding an inch in thickness, was affixed to one end of his hemp cable to facilitate its transport across the Niagara River. On the American side, the cable was coiled around an oak tree in White's Pleasure Grounds. However, securing it on the Canadian side posed a challenge. Blondin's assistants harbored concerns that the delicate rope might not withstand the weight of the cable as it was hoisted up the gorge for anchorage in Canada. Yet, to the amusement of his spectators, the tightrope walker devised a bold and audacious solution.

Securing another rope around his waist, he descended a staggering 200 feet along the slender rope, affixed the second rope to the end of the cable, and then calmly ascended back to Canadian soil, where he firmly anchored the cable to a sturdy rock. To minimize sway, guy ropes were strategically positioned at 20-foot intervals along the cable, extending to posts on both banks, resembling a colossal spider web. Nevertheless, Blondin could not rectify the unavoidable sag in the cable's center, spanning approximately 50 feet, where it proved impossible to affix guy ropes. This meant he would be 190 feet above the gaping gorge during his crossing's midpoint. Many onlookers felt certain that he was walking towards his own demise.

Shortly before 5 p.m., Blondin positioned himself on the American side, wearing pink tights covered with sparkles, and the sun reflected off his tights, giving him an otherworldly glow. His footwear consisted of supple leather shoes with gentle soles, and he wielded a balance pole crafted from ash, measuring 26 feet in length and weighing close to 50 pounds. With deliberate poise, he commenced his journey. "His stride," remarked one observer, "resembled that of a proud rooster in a barnyard." Children clung tightly to their mothers' legs while women peered cautiously behind their parasols. Several spectators succumbed to fainting spells. Astonishing the crowd, Blondin halted about a third of the way across, seated himself on the cable, and signaled for the Maid of the Mist, the renowned tourist vessel, to anchor beneath him briefly. Lowering a line, he retrieved a bottle of wine, indulged in a sip, and then resumed his journey, picking up pace after surpassing the sagging midpoint. Accompanied by the strains of "Home, Sweet Home" played by the band, Blondin reached Canadian soil. Assisted by a bystander, he was brought ashore, prompting one witness to exclaim, "I wouldn't endure such a sight again for all the riches in the world."

Following a brief 20-minute break, Blondin embarked on his journey to the opposite side, carrying a Daguerreotype camera. He traversed 200 feet along the cable carefully before securing his balance pole and unloading the camera. He captured a stunning photograph of the crowd gathered on the American side with precision before reattaching the camera and resuming his journey across. The entire spectacle took only 23 minutes, and Blondin wasted no time announcing an eagerly awaited encore performance scheduled for the Fourth of July.

Blondin's feat didn't garner universal admiration. The New York Times criticized the "reckless and purposeless endangerment of life" and condemned the "careless spectators" who found entertainment in watching "a fellow human in mortal danger." Mark Twain later disparaged Blondin as "that adventurous fool." One resident of Niagara Falls went so far as to claim Blondin was a hoax, insisting that such a person didn't exist. Despite the skepticism, on July 4, Blondin returned to the American end of the cable, this time without his balancing pole. Midway, he lay on the cable, flipped over, and walked backward. Pausing to take a swig from his flask, he safely reached the Canadian side. For the return journey, he donned a sack over his body, depriving himself of sight.

Blondin's death-defying feats of tightrope walking across Niagara Falls drew large crowds eager to witness his incredible stunts. His performances only grew more daring over time, culminating in a series of impressive crossings that stunned even the most seasoned onlookers. In one such event, with President Millard Fillmore watching, Blondin walked backward to Canada and back while pushing a wheelbarrow. Not content to stop there, he then performed somersaults and backflips while traversing the cable, often pausing to dangle from it with just one hand. Despite a few guy ropes snapping along the way, Blondin proved fearless, making multiple successful crossings, even carrying Harry Colcord on his back during one of them.

Blondin's daring feats continued to captivate audiences worldwide. He crossed the falls at night with a locomotive headlight affixed to each end of the cable. He crossed while his body was in shackles. He even attempted to carry a table and chair, intending to sit down in the middle, but the chair fell into the water. Despite the mishap, Blondin remained composed, sat on the cable, and enjoyed a piece of cake with champagne. In one of his most famous stunts, he carried a stove and utensils on his back, started a fire in the center of the cable, and cooked an omelet. Once ready, he lowered the breakfast to passengers on the Maid of the Mist deck.

Blondin's performances took him to various countries, including China, Japan, Australia, India, and across Europe. However, he became disillusioned with America in 1888 when he was prohibited from performing in Central Park and had to settle for St. George in Staten Island. Despite being 65 years old at the time, he carried his son and another man on his back and cooked another omelet for the crowd. By his final performance in 1896, Blondin had crossed Niagara Falls an estimated 300 times and walked over 10,000 miles on his rope. He passed away the following year due to complications from diabetes, having never had life insurance throughout his nearly 73 years on Earth. As he often joked, no one would dare take such a risk.

THE U.S. GOVERNMENT TRIED TO MAKE IT RAIN BY EXPLODING DYNAMITE IN THE SKY

Edward Powers, a former Civil War general, observed in his 1871 book, "War and the Weather," noting that rain often followed Civil War battles. He theorized that the loud noise of battle agitated clouds, causing them to release stored rain. Powers documented several historical battles and their subsequent rain events in his book. Plutarch, an ancient Greek essayist from the second century, had noted that rainfall frequently occurred after battles, lending credence to the concussion theory. Napoleon himself tried to trigger rain by firing artillery into the sky.

On August 17, 1891, a team of scientists embarked on the inaugural government-funded rainmaking experiments. Under the leadership of Robert G. Dyrenforth, they journeyed from Washington, D.C., to a Texas cattle ranch equipped with dynamite, kites, and balloons, the necessary apparatus for their rain-inducing project. Adhering to the concussion theory of weather manipulation, which proposed that loud sounds could trigger rainfall by unsettling clouds, and the scientists readied explosives for detonation.

Two decades after Powers released his book, Senator Charles B. Farwell of Illinois, an advocate for rainmaking, sought $10,000 from the Senate Appropriations Committee to support rainmaking initiatives. Initially removed by the House, the Senate later restored the request, ultimately assigning $7,000 for the experiments to be conducted within the Department of Agriculture's Forestry Division.

Dyrenforth, a patent lawyer from Washington, D.C., led the experiments, assisted by meteorologist George E. Curtis, chemist Claude O. Rosell, and John T. Ellis from Oberlin College.

Originating from Chicago, Dyrenforth pursued his studies in Germany, where he enrolled at the Polytechnic School in Karlsruhe and later earned a mechanical engineering degree from the University of Heidelberg. His involvement as a war correspondent during the 1861 Austro-Prussian war, coupled with his service as a major in the Union Army during the American Civil War, constituted pivotal periods in his biography. Transitioning into the realm of patent law, Dyrenforth delved into numerous applications for rain-making inventions from clients, gradually fostering a personal fixation with the idea.

The inaugural experiment led by Dyrenforth's team

unfolded at what they designated as the "C" ranch, situated on land near Midland owned by Chicago's prominent meat-packing figure, Nelson Morris. Roughly twelve hours after triggering the initial round of explosives, rain commenced. Despite the modest amount of rainfall collected at the ranch, Dyrenforth interpreted it as an indication of success.

Following this, they proceeded with the subsequent round of explosions, employing 156 pounds of rackarock (a type of explosive) on August 21, coinciding with the arrival of a "norther" or a cold front known for inducing precipitation in the region. Hours after the cessation of explosions, mist emerged, prompting Dyrenforth to attribute the outcome to their actions.

The final experiment at the ranch was on August 25, with explosions done throughout the day. Dyrenforth reported the occurrence of rainfall around 3:00 a.m. But no one measured the rain, and observers later said it was only a sprinkle.

The prevalent perspective shared even among officials at the recently established U.S. Weather Bureau, and others were marked by considerable skepticism regarding the notion of enhancing rainfall from clouds through the utilization of explosive devices, as there was no credible scientific foundation for such practices.

Among the skeptics was the team's meteorologist, George E. Curtis of the Smithsonian, who departed from the group a day prior to the final experiment. Upon returning to Washington, Curtis maintained that the experiments lacked scientific validity.

However, Dyrenforth, among specific individuals, remained convinced that concussion experiments could have been effective. When the mayor of El Paso, Texas, extended an invitation for the rainmakers to trial their methods in the arid desert town, Dyrenforth dispatched his team under the leadership of John T. Ellis to conduct experiments there. Supported financially by El Paso, Ellis and the rainmakers procured six dozen bombshell salutes, 2,000 cubic feet (about twice the volume of a small semi-truck) of oxygen, and 1,000 pounds of dynamite. The day before the test, Ellis filled a balloon with hydrogen and let it float into the clouds as artillerists fired the explosives.

Later that night, rainfall was observed south and southeast of the city. Although the rainmakers conducted experiments on the opposite side of town, they claimed credit for the showers. Subsequently, the rainmakers conducted experiments in Corpus Christi, San Antonio, and San Diego, yielding similar inconclusive results. It has been noted that meteorologists had forecasted rain in all these locations on the days when the rainmakers attempted to induce precipitation from the clouds. Nevertheless, Dyrenforth and his team conducted their experiments during the southwest's traditional rainy season, suggesting that rainfall was probable regardless.

Ten years later, Charles W. Post, the breakfast cereal magnate, conducted his own experiments in Texas's Garza and Lynn counties. Over several hours, he detonated four-pound dynamite charges every four minutes. However, his experiments between 1910 and 1914 yielded inconclusive results, marking the end of the concussion experiments era.

Although the concussion theory has fallen out of favor, the science of rainmaking continues to progress. Today, researchers studying weather modification concentrate on cloud seeding.

This process involves introducing silver iodide crystals into clouds to encourage ice droplets to merge and precipitate. Cloud seeding shows promise, but its effectiveness remains somewhat uncertain as science continues to develop.

ANCIENT GREEK AND ROMAN STATUS WEREN'T ORIGINALLY WHITE

In ancient times, as one approached the grand Temple of Aphaia located on the Greek island of Aegina, they would have been greeted by a sculpture depicting a young archer, meticulously painted in vibrant colors to render a lifelike appearance. Accounts from the period, including writings by the Roman author Pliny the Elder, attest to the practice of painting sculptures in ancient Greece rather than leaving them in the natural white marble state. The notion of the classical period, characterized by the artistic and philosophical excellence of ancient Greece and Rome, has its origins, to a large extent, in the Neoclassical era. The resurgence of interest in antiquity took some time to reach its peak, particularly during the 18th century, when allusions to Greek and Latin rhetoric, architecture, and sculpture pervaded cultural discourse. However, from the

Renaissance onwards, the classical ethos attained the status of cultural orthodoxy.

One aspect of classical idealism perpetuated a misconception that Roman and Greek sculpture epitomized an ideal of pristine whiteness. This misinterpretation endured for centuries as modern sculptors crafted busts and statues from polished white marble. However, historical accuracy reveals that both Greek and Roman statues originally boasted vibrant, colorful adornments.

Nevertheless, many contemporary individuals express surprise upon learning about the vivid colors adorning classical statues. How and why did the myth of colorless marble statues originate? The assumption arose because the original colors on most ancient statues were faded and chipped off by the time they were unburied, leading to the belief that they had always been devoid of color. This misconception likely stemmed from a desire to appreciate white marble's perceived simplicity and purity, aligning with prevailing notions of superiority associated with white people, which were prevalent during that period.

The excavation of Pompeii in the 18th century was expected to provide evidence that painting statues in the ancient world was a common practice. However, this expectation was not fulfilled despite the city's destruction by a volcanic eruption in 79 A.D., which preserved many statues with paint still on them, such as a statue of the Greek goddess Artemis.

One notable instance where traces of color were discovered is the "Peplos Kore," which is currently housed in Athens' Acropolis Museum. Unearthed during extensive excavations of the Acropolis in Greece in the 19th century, this marble sculpture dates back to the Archaic period around 530 B.C. It originates from the Greek island of Paros. Traces of orange coloring were found on the figure's locks of hair. However, upon noticing these remnants of paint, archaeologists promptly created casts from which they produced white plaster replicas of the statue. These replicas were then distributed to international expositions, perpetuating the misconception that ancient Greek statues were predominantly white.

In the 20th century, fascist regimes appropriated the concept of white figures from antiquity as a symbol of white superiority. Leaders such as Benito Mussolini and Adolf Hitler admired the art and architecture of ancient Greece and Rome, utilizing the notion of white classical statues to reinforce ideas of racial supremacy. For the Nazis, this involved associating the image of the imaginary Aryan race with Greek statues, emphasizing features such as finely sculpted torsos as exemplars of their perceived racial ideals.

PASS THE CORNCOB, WOULD YA?

Before the advent of mass-produced, commercially available toilet paper in the mid-1800s and the subsequent ongoing improvements into the early 20th century, people relied on less sophisticated methods for personal hygiene.

Throughout history, local customs and climatic conditions often dictated the methods used for anal hygiene. Additionally, social hierarchy played a significant role in shaping toilet habits. What remains evident is that humans across different eras and cultures employed various natural tools and materials for cleansing. In ancient times, practices included wiping with stones and other organic items, supplemented by rinsing with water or snow. Some cultures favored the use of seashells and animal furs for this purpose.

During the first century A.D., Romans utilized a communal sponge attached to a stick for personal hygiene. These sponges, referred to as tersoriums, were either employed once and then cleaned in a solution of vinegar or salt water for reuse, or they functioned akin to toilet brushes rather than toilet paper.

Apart from the communal sponge, Greco-Romans also utilized moss, leaves, and pieces of ceramic known as pessoi for cleansing purposes. Pessoi fragments might have originated from ostraca, which were broken pieces of pottery, often bearing the names of adversaries.

In 1992, archaeologists unearthed hygiene sticks dating back 2,000 years at Xuanquanzhi, a former Han Dynasty military outpost along the Silk Road in China. These implements, known as salaka, cechou, and chugi, were crafted from bamboo and other woods, resembling spatulas. Their ends were wrapped in cloth and harbored traces of preserved fecal matter.

By the early 14th century, the Chinese had established a robust toilet paper production, churning out between 10 million packages containing 1,000 to 10,000 sheets annually. In 1393, the Hongwu Emperor's imperial family received thousands of scented paper sheets.

While paper became widely accessible in the 15th century, modern commercially available toilet paper didn't emerge in the Western world until 1857. Joseph Gayetty of New York introduced "Medicated Paper, for the Water-Closet," retailed in packages of 500 sheets for 50 cents. Before Gayetty's innovation, Americans resorted to improvisations.

Throughout the 1700s, corncobs served as a common alternative to toilet paper. Subsequently, newspapers and magazines became prevalent in the early 18th and 19th centuries. The first perforated toilet paper rolls made their debut in 1890, and by 1930, toilet paper was finally manufactured "splinter-free." Additionally, colored toilet paper was available from the 1950s through the 1980s, allowing consumers to coordinate with their bathroom decor.

PIGS....IN.....SPACE.....

D espite her notoriety, Laika the dog was not the inaugural animal sent into space; both NASA and the Soviet Union had been launching animals for roughly a decade before her mission. Nonetheless, Laika holds the distinction of being the first living being to achieve orbit around Earth following her historic launch on November 3, 1957.

The initial occupants of space were fruit flies. On February 20, 1947, the United States dispatched fruit flies aboard confiscated German V-2 rockets to investigate radiation exposure at high altitudes. In a mere 3 minutes and 10 seconds of flight, the fruit flies ascended to an altitude of 68 miles.

On June 14, 1949, NASA sent a rhesus monkey named Albert II into space, making him the first mammal to do so. Despite being anesthetized and outfitted with sensors to track his health, Albert tragically did not survive the trip back down to Earth.

While the United States opted for monkeys as substitutes for humans on their early space flights, the Soviet Union utilized dogs. The inaugural canine spacefarers, Tsygan and Dezik, embarked on the R-1 IIIA-1 mission. On July 22, 1951, these dogs ascended into space, albeit without achieving orbit. They marked the first mammals to be successfully retrieved from spaceflight.

Though the boundary between Earth's atmosphere and outer space lacks a definitive boundary, scientists commonly recognize an imaginary line approximately 68 miles (110 kilometers) from the planet's surface, known as the Karman line, as the threshold. In 1957, Laika, an intrepid mixed-breed stray, captured the world's attention as the first animal to orbit Earth. Despite her heroic journey and the groundbreaking scientific achievement it represented, Laika's tragic fate remains a sad reminder of the dangers of space exploration. Dubbed "Muttnik" by American journalists in a playful nod to the Soviet Union's recent launch of Sputnik, Laika's story remains a poignant example of the sacrifices made in the pursuit of scientific progress.

The Soviet Union launched the first mammals to orbit Earth and return safely on August 19, 1960, as part of the Sputnik 5 mission. Among the notable passengers were Belka and Strelka, two Soviet space dogs. Additionally, the flight carried a variety of creatures, including one rabbit, forty mice, two rats, and fifteen containers of fruit flies.

In 1968, two steppe tortoises made history by becoming the first animals to circumnavigate the moon aboard the Soviet Zond 5 mission, which achieved the first successful orbit around the moon. Despite the tortoises surviving the journey, they were later dissected upon their return to Earth for comparative studies with their terrestrial counterparts, aiming to uncover any effects of spaceflight.

During the early stages of space exploration, scientists and engineers employed animals, particularly dogs, monkeys, and chimps, to gather insights into launching and safely returning living organisms from space. These endeavors aimed to enhance understanding of spaceflight's potential impacts on the human body.

NAPOLEON WASN'T FRENCH

D espite being widely renowned as a prominent figure in world history, Napoleon Bonaparte was not of French descent. In fact, Napoleon hailed from Italian ancestry. His paternal lineage, the Buonapartes, originated from a minor Tuscan noble family that relocated to Corsica in the 16th century. In contrast, his maternal lineage, the Ramolinos, stemmed from a lesser-known Genoese noble family.

Napoleon was born shortly after the Republic of Genoa relinquished control of Corsica to France. The island was annexed by France in the year of his birth, following a period during which it had been sold off and had experienced both independence and Genoese rule spanning five centuries. Despite his imminent arrival, Napoleon's parents were actively involved in Corsican resistance efforts against the French occupation, with his mother Maria even participating in the resistance while pregnant.

His father, Carlo, initially aligned himself with patriot Pasquale Paoli during Corsica's struggle for independence from

France. However, following the Corsican defeat at Ponte Novu in 1769 and Paoli's exile in Britain, Carlo transitioned to working for the newly established French administration. In 1777, he was appointed as the island's representative to the court of Louis XVI.

He harbored resentment towards the French monarchy and threw his support behind the French Revolution in 1789 while serving within the French army, endeavoring to propagate its principles in his native Corsica. His ascent through the military ranks was swift, notably when he intervened to save the governing French Directory from royalist insurgents. In 1796, he launched a successful military campaign against the Austrians and their Italian allies, achieving decisive victories that propelled him to national hero status. Just two years later, he spearheaded an army expedition to Egypt, leveraging it as a platform for political ascendancy. Seizing the opportunity, he orchestrated a coup in November 1799 and assumed the role of First Consul of the Republic. By 1804, in a bid to centralize and extend his authority, he proclaimed himself Emperor of the French. His reign as Emperor endured from 1804 until 1814, with a brief return in 1815.

SACAJAWEA WAS PREGNANT WHILE SHE LED LEWIS AND CLARK ACROSS AMERICA

S ix months pregnant at the outset of the Lewis and Clark expedition, Sacagawea, the Shoshone interpreter and guide, experienced the birth of her first child, Jean Baptiste Charbonneau, during the journey.

Meriwether Lewis and William Clark initially encountered the youthful Sacagawea while wintering among the Mandan tribe near the Upper Missouri River, near present-day Bismarck, North Dakota. Despite her tender age, Sacagawea was wedded to a French-Canadian fur trapper named Toussaint Charbonneau, who had acquired her from Hidatsa captors a year earlier. The Hidatsa took Sacagawea from her homeland along the Continental Divide in southwestern Montana and southeastern Idaho, and Sacagawea was descended from a notable Shoshone leader. The Hidatsa viewed captives like her as mere workers and promptly sold

E.D. GARNER

Sacagawea and another woman to Charbonneau, who engaged them in various duties, including labor and companionship.

During that winter, Lewis and Clark enlisted Charbonneau as an interpreter for their forthcoming journey to the Pacific and back if he brought his youthful wife. Recognizing the necessity of acquiring horses from the Shoshone to traverse the Continental Divide, Lewis and Clark understood the potential value of Sacagawea's assistance as an interpreter. With Charbonneau's consent, she thus became the sole woman to accompany the Corps of Discovery.

Two months before the expedition's departure, Lewis and Clark unexpectedly found themselves with another companion, who would later prove invaluable in an unforeseen manner. On this particular day in 1805, Sacagawea went into labor. Lewis, who would assume the role of the expedition's doctor in the months ahead, was summoned for the first and only time during the journey to assist in the delivery. Anxious to ensure the well-being of their new Shoshone interpreter for the challenging journey ahead, Lewis later recounted that her labor was long and painful. Advised that a small dose of rattlesnake rattler might expedite the delivery, Lewis crushed up a portion of the rattler tail and mixed it with water. "She had not consumed (the mixture) for more than ten minutes before giving birth," Lewis joyfully reported.

The arrival of a new member of the Corps of Discovery was marked by the joyful cries of a healthy young boy named Jean Baptiste Charbonneau. Despite the challenges of the journey, no one ever considered leaving Sacagawea and her newborn son behind. In April 1805, Sacagawea carried Jean Baptiste on her back in an Indian cradleboard as the party set out up the Missouri.

Clark, who developed a strong connection with the child, affectionately nicknamed him "Pomp" or "Pompey." Jean Baptiste accompanied his mother on her remarkable journey to the Pacific and back every step of the way.

Both mother and son proved indispensable to the expedition. As anticipated, Sacagawea's skill as a translator proved crucial in obtaining horses from the Shoshone. Additionally, Jean Baptiste's presence unexpectedly reassured the Native Americans they encountered of the expedition's peaceful intentions. The sight of a mother with her infant led the Indians to conclude that the party was not a war party, as no such group would include a vulnerable child.

Upon the Corps of Discovery's return to the East in 1805, Charbonneau, Sacagawea, and Jean Baptiste went back to their lives in the fur trading industry. Sacagawea's subsequent fate remains largely unknown, although reports suggest she succumbed to a "putrid fever" in 1812 at a trading post along the Missouri River. Honoring a pledge he made to Sacagawea during the expedition, Clark financed Jean Baptiste's education at a Catholic academy in St. Louis and assumed a paternal role in his life. Jean Baptiste, a gifted and charming individual, mastered French, German, and Spanish, engaged in hunting expeditions with European aristocrats in the Black Forest of Germany, embarked on journeys to Africa and later ventured into further exploration of the American West. He passed away in 1866 while on the way to Montana's newly discovered gold fields.

BIBLIOGRAPHY

Don't Just Take My Word For It:

Want To Know More About One Of The Fascinating Stories In This Book? If So, Try One Of These History Books For A Deep Dive Into The Subject You Are Interested In.

Berkin, Carol. *A Sovereign People: The Crises of the 1790s and the Birth of American Nationalism.* New York: Basic Books, 2017.

Bissell, William Cunningham. *Urban Design, Chaos, and Colonial Power in Zanzibar.* Bloomington: Indiana University Press, 2010.

Blaufarb, Rafe. *Napoleon: Symbol for an Age, A Brief History with Documents.* Bedford, 2008.

Burgess, Colin. *Animals in Space: From Research Rockets to the Space Shuttle.* Springer, 2007.

Dash, Mike. *Tulipomania: The Story of the World's Most Coveted Flower and the Extraordinary Passions It Aroused.* Crown Publishing, 1999.

Fischer, Paul. *The Man Who Invented Motion Pictures: A True Tale of Obsession, Murder, and the Movies.* Simon & Schuster, 2022.

Fleming, James. *Fixing the Sky: The Checkered History of Weather and Climate Control.* Columbia University Press, 2010.

Hibbert, Christopher. *The Days of the French Revolution.* William Morrow Paperbacks, 2012.

Hutton, Ronald. *The Making of Oliver Cromwell.* Yale University Press, 2022.

Kimmel, Elizabeth Cody. *Before Columbus: The Leif Eriksson Expedition: A True Adventure.* New York: Random House, 2003.

Marvel, William. *Andersonville: The Last Depot.* Chapel Hill: University of North Carolina Press, 1995.

McGreevy, Patrick. Imagining Niagara: The Meaning and Making of Niagara Falls. University of Massachusetts Press, 1994.

Means, Howard. *Johnny Appleseed: The Man, the Myth, the American Story.* New York: Simon & Schuster, 2011.

Moyer, Paul B. *Detestable and Wicked Arts: New England and Witchcraft in the Early Modern Atlantic World.* Ithaca: Cornell University Press, 2020.

Peralta, Dan-el Padilla, Matthew P. Loar, Carolyn MacDonald, editors. *Rome, Empire of Plunder: The Dynamics of Cultural Appropriation.* Cambridge University Press, 2017.

Rabinovitch-Fox, Einav. *Dressed for Freedom: The Fashionable Politics of American Feminism.* University of Illinois Press, 2021.

Spivey, Nigel. *The Ancient Olympics.* Oxford University Press, 2012.

Sugg, Richard. *Mummies, Cannibals, and Vampires: The History of Corpse Medicine from the Renaissance to the Victorians.* New York: Routledge, 2016.

Taylor, David. *The New Police in Nineteenth-Century England: Crime, Conflict, and Control.* Manchester, UK: Manchester University Press, 1997.

Werbel, Amy. *Lust on Trial: Censorship and the Rise of American Obscenity in the Age of Anthony Comstock.* New York: Columbia University Press, 2018.

Westad, Odd Arne. *The Cold War: A World History.* New York:

Hatchett Books, 2017.

Wynbrandt, James. *The Excruciating History of Dentistry: Toothsome Tales & Oral Oddities from Babylon to Braces*. St. Martin's Griffin, 2000.

ABOUT THE AUTHOR

E. D. Garner

E.D. Garner teaches history at a small college in upstate New York and is a historical reenactor on the weekends.

Follow the author bio page for new and exciting books in this growing series.

Made in the USA
Coppell, TX
05 December 2024

41831446R00066